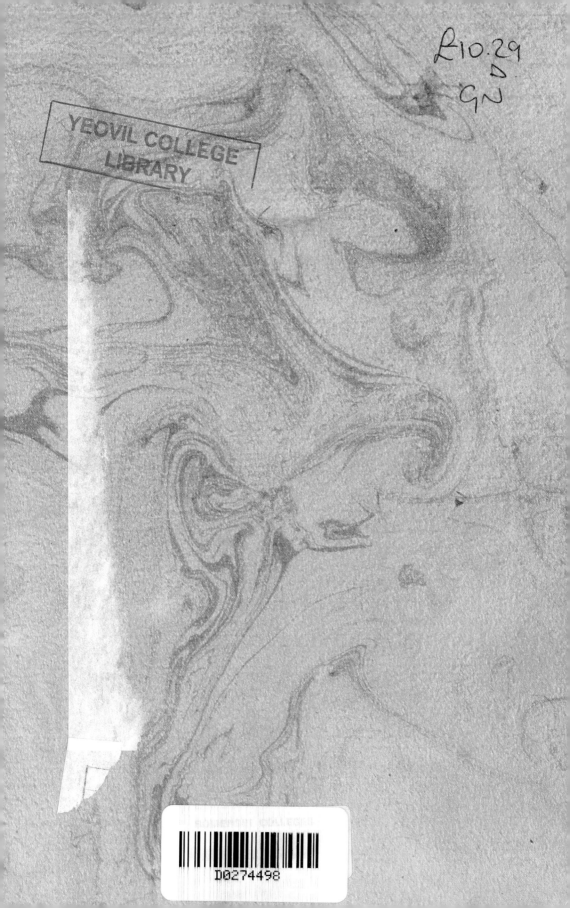

MAKING YOUR OWN
PAPER

MARIANNE SADDINGTON

Photographs by Juan Espi
Illustrations by Marianne Saddington

A Storey Publishing Book

STOREY

Storey Communications, Inc.
Schoolhouse Road
Pownal, Vermont 05261

United States edition published in 1992 by Storey Communications, Inc., Schoolhouse Road, Pownal, Vermont 05261.
United Kingdom edition published in 1991 by New Holland (Publishers) Ltd, 37 Connaught Street, London W2 2AZ.

Reprinted in 1993

Storey Communications, Inc. editors: Gwen W. Steege, Elizabeth P. Stell
Designer: Janice Evans
Cover designer: Abdul Amien
Storey Communications, Inc. text designer: Michelle M. Arabia
Photographic stylist: Elaine Levitte
Indexer: Linda de Villiers

Typeset by Diatype Setting cc
Reproduction by Hirt & Carter (Pty) Ltd
Printed and bound in Singapore by Kyodo Printing Co (Singapore) Pte Ltd

The information in this book is true and complete to the best of our knowledge. All recommendations are made without guarantee on the part of the author or Storey Communications, Inc. The author and publisher disclaim any liability in connection with the use of this information. For additional information please contact Storey Communications, Inc., Schoolhouse Road, Pownal, Vermont 05261.

Library of Congress Cataloging-in-Publication Data

Saddington, Marianne.
   Making your own paper / Marianne Saddington ; photographs by Juan Espar ; illustrations by Marianne Saddington.
                    p.   cm.
   Originally published: Cape Town : Struikhof Publishers, 1990.
   Includes bibliographical references and index.
   ISBN 0-88266-784-X (pbk)
   1. Papermaking.   2. Paper, Handmade.   3. Paper work.
I. Espi, Juan.   II. Title.
[TS1105.S17   1992]
676'.22—dc20
91-41503

Title page: Paper-cast of an African mask, woodcut (by Thelma Harwood) and paper-cast of clay mold.

Contents

Introduction

As a calligrapher, I was initially attracted to paper-making in order to make, and write on, interesting and unusual paper. Once introduced to the technique, I was amazed at its simplicity. This led to a deep involvement in its history and a love of its variety and textural richness. The beauty of handmade paper is that no two sheets are alike.

With such a range of commercial papers available today, what is the attraction of making one's own? Many people enjoy handmade things. The unique texture and individual quality of handmade paper turns it into more than just a surface to write or draw on — it is an object of beauty in its own right.

Recycling wastepaper is a useful and relatively cheap way to reduce waste in our 'throw-away' society. Hunting for the raw materials used to make paper, or growing them in your garden, can also be exciting.

Paper-making need not be expensive, unless you want to make cotton paper or experiment with Japanese methods. All you need is a flat surface, access to water, an electric blender, absorbent fabric, a few hand tools and raw materials from your kitchen or garden.

Paper is such a commonplace thing, yet few people are familiar with paper-making techniques. These techniques are in fact very simple, allowing the amateur to make unusual and individual papers in a relatively short time. This book provides basic information about the processes involved in making paper, and gives simplified versions of both traditional and modern methods. It starts off with simple methods of recycling used paper, and progresses to making paper from various cultivated plants. Projects at the end of each chapter will increase your expertise and confidence, and spur you on to experiments of your own. There are also ideas for turning paper into creative gifts for family and friends, and for exploring the possibilities of paper art.

From left to right: vellum, Egyptian papyrus, beaten hibiscus bark, bark paper from Uganda and Japanese paper.

Chapter 1
What is paper?

'To be classed as true paper the thin sheets must be made from fiber that has been macerated until each individual filament is a separate unit; the fibers intermixed with water, and by the use of a sieve-like screen, the fibers lifted from the water in the form of a thin stratum, the water draining through the small openings of the screen, leaving a sheet of matted fiber upon the screen's surface. This thin layer of intertwined fiber is paper.'

DARD HUNTER, 1978

Essentially paper consists of the bonded fibers of plant material such as wood, straw, flax, hemp or cotton which is shredded, broken down to expose the cellulose in the fibers, then beaten to a pulp and mixed with water. If this mixture is drained through a sieve, the layer of fibrous material remaining on the sieve will dry to form paper. While making spinach soup, for example, you could produce a coarse sheet of spinach paper. If, after boiling and blending the spinach, you pour the pulpy mixture through a sieve, the thin, 'smoother' pulp will drain away (to be used for the soup), while the coarser material will remain in the sieve, forming a thin layer of matted fibers on the mesh. This layer of plant matter will dry into paper.

Paper as we know it today originated in China about two thousand years ago. Its invention is usually attributed to a Chinese eunuch, Ts'ai Lun, in A.D.105, although earlier examples have been recorded. Previously, Chinese scribes wrote on strips of wood or bamboo with a pointed stylus, but this was cumbersome and the strips of wood or bamboo were succeeded by books and scrolls of woven cloth. Ts'ai Lun took the idea a step further and began making paper from the bark of trees, hemp waste, old rags, fish nets and other plant fibers.

Since then many other plants have been used to make paper, including mulberry bark, hemp, China grass, bamboo and gampi. When paper was finally introduced to Europe a thousand years later, many of these plants were unavailable there, and most European paper was initially made from linen and cotton rags. The development of the printing trade increased the need for larger quantities of paper and at the beginning of the 19th century there was a search for a more economical and plentiful raw material. This discovery led to the use of refined wood pulp to make paper.

The use of wood in paper-making was not new. It was first suggested to a French naturalist, de Réaumur, by his observations of the age-old nest-building activities of the wasp. The

Wasp's nest and dried wood pulp.

wasp rasps dry wood and chews it into a workable paste with which it makes a papery nest that is tough and highly water-resistant. This discovery later led chemists to experiment with the properties of wood as a substance for making paper.

The bulk of our paper today is made from chemically and mechanically refined wood pulp sprayed onto fast-moving belts of felt. Essentially the preparation and techniques are the same as for handmade paper, which was almost totally replaced by mass-production methods some 200 years ago.

In general artists still prefer handmade paper because of its strength and long-lasting qualities. In the West these properties are principally the result of a high cotton content. Cotton fibers are long, strong and resistant to the long-term destructive effects of light and atmosphere. The higher the percentage of cotton (and the lower the percentage of wood pulp) in the paper, the higher its quality. In the East the slow, gentle processing of long-fiberd plants creates thin papers of remarkable tensile strength and durability.

What cannot be classed as paper?

Several substances we loosely classify as 'paper' cannot be regarded as true paper at all, for example papyrus, rice paper, parchment, vellum and the traditional bark papers of Central America and Polynesia.

Papyrus is a laminated material and not true paper, and was made from the plant *Cyperus papyrus* which grew abundantly on the banks of the Nile. Papyrus was prepared by slicing longitudinal strips from the inner stems of these plants, arranging them side by side in two or three layers, crosswise and lengthwise, soaking them in water and pressing them into a smooth surface.

Rice paper is a misnomer on two counts — it is neither made of rice, nor is it true paper. It is made from a tree, *Tetrapanex papyriferum* (formerly *Fatsia papyrifera*), which grows in the hills of northern Taiwan. Using a sharp knife, the 'paper' is cut spirally from the inner pitch of the plant's stem.

Parchment and vellum as writing surfaces date back to at least 1500 B.C. and are still used today for diplomas and special manuscripts. Although they feel and look like paper, they are made from the stretched and treated skins of sheep and calves. Parchment is made from the fleshy side of the split skin of a sheep (strong leather is obtained from the wool side), while

Making papyrus.

Slicing the outer green skin off the stem.

Layers of thin slices of pith are placed on top of each other at right angles.

Beating the layers gently with a mallet to facilitate bonding of the fibers.

vellum is made from the whole skin of still-born or newly born calves or lambs.

The original inhabitants of Mexico, Central America and Polynesia used the beaten inner bark of the hemp plant and fig and mulberry branches to make a type of paper called huun, amatl and tapa.

Chapter 2
How to begin

The simplest way to make paper is to recycle wastepaper, for example computer paper or notepaper, by blending it with water to form a pulp. Having made enough pulp to form a few sheets of paper, a frame is placed on top of a piece of thick cloth, usually dressmakers' felt or old woolen blankets, and the pulp poured over the felt within the frame. The water is then removed by allowing it to drain and by placing a dry piece of felt on top of the wet paper to absorb excess water. A rolling pin can be used to remove even more water by rolling it firmly over the top piece of felt. The felt with its wet paper can then be hung up to dry. This chapter also includes information on how to store left-over pulp. To get started, make your first few sheets of paper by reading the instructions and carrying out the first two projects.

Basic equipment needed to make paper using the pouring method. *Clockwise from top right:* large plastic bottle, frames, embroidery frame, sponge, wooden spoon, jug, rolling pin, funnel, colander with netting and bucket.

Basic equipment for the pouring method

Frame (small picture or embroidery frame, chopsticks, strips of wood or pieces of cardboard bent into a rectangular frame) in which to pour the paper pulp. The size should be approximately 8" x 6".

Absorbent sponge for mopping water

Jug or large milk carton for pouring pulp

Wooden spoon for stirring pulp

Rolling pin or smooth glass bottle (a wine bottle, for example) for pressing the wet paper sheets to remove excess water

Plastic bucket for storing pulp

Large plastic bottle for storing pulp

Funnel for draining leftover pulp

Electric blender for beating (or macerating) plant fibers into the pulp that will form paper. Traditionally the Japanese pounded their plants by hand with wooden mallets. For the purposes of this book, a kitchen blender with a capacity of about 1 quart is an adequate substitute.

Felt on which to pour the pulp to form sheets of paper. Traditionally felted woolen cloth was used, but dressmakers' felt works well and is easily obtainable at fabric stores. Use only the thinner natural fiber felt, not the thicker polyester variety. Manmade chamois cloths, old woolen blankets, cotton sheeting or thick calico can also be used, but avoid thin fabrics — the 'felt' must have a certain stiffness. (However, for the project at the end of this chapter you will be using cotton fabric instead of felt, as you will be ironing the paper dry.)

Net curtaining and colander to drain leftover pulp. Such pulp can be stored in sealed buckets or bottles as is, or drained through a sieve or colander lined with mesh to reduce the bulk and facilitate storing (*see* p. 19 for further details). You can also use a cut-off nylon stocking for this purpose, or make a useful net drainage bag that fits a standard size bucket.

How to make a drainage bag
Cut a piece of net curtaining 28" x 40". Machine stitch the two shorter sides together, creating a

tube, and then sew the bottom of the bag in the same way. Turn down 1½ inches at the top of the bag, fold under the raw edge and machine stitch.

Net bag to fit a standard-sized bucket.

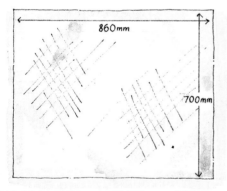

Net curtaining. (700 mm = 28"; 860 mm = 40")

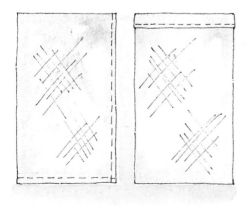

Sew sides and bottom seams.

Turn down top and hem.

How to make pulp

Recycled paper pulp can be made from tissues, computer paper, photocopying paper, wrapping-paper, brown paper, artists' watercolor paper, pastel paper, notepaper or envelopes, used on their own or in combination. Do not use heavily printed paper if you want to make long-lasting paper (*see* box below), and cut out and discard those parts of the paper with adhesive tape, glue, plastic or staples.

> **Note:** *Newspapers and magazines can be recycled, but must be boiled in detergent to remove the ink. Tear the paper into strips and boil it for about an hour in a solution of one tablespoon of dish detergent to 2 quarts of water. Remove the scum that rises to the surface while boiling — this is the ink being lifted off the paper. After boiling, rinse the paper well before blending it to make pulp. There are some disadvantages to recycling newspaper — the paper is prone to acid attack, deteriorates rapidly and becomes brittle and yellow with age because of the impurities left in the original pulp by the processing method. It can be interesting to recycle newspapers as an experiment, but never use it to make long-lasting paper.*

First tear the paper into pieces measuring approximately 1 inch square and soak in water overnight. The better the quality of the paper, the smaller you need to tear the pieces and the longer they must be soaked. For example, tissues can be torn into quite large pieces and soaked for only 30 minutes, while Fabriano watercolor paper needs to be torn into pieces less than 1 inch square, and soaked for two to three days. You can speed up the process by pouring boiling water over the torn paper and allowing it to stand. Most paper will then be ready to macerate after an hour or two.

Once the paper has been soaked, it is macerated in an electric blender or food processor. Place a small handful of wet, torn paper and two cups of water in a blender, and blend for 15-30 seconds. Thick cardboard or quality papers will take longer. After a while, experience will tell you how long to blend different kinds of paper. It is best to blend the paper for the *shortest possible time* — just long enough for the fibers to separate. Stop the machine after 15 seconds and check: if there are still large pieces of paper visible, allow another ten seconds and check it again. Do not worry about little bits that do not break down entirely, as they can add character to the paper.

If you do not have a blender, you can beat the soaked paper strips into pulp by pounding them in a bucket with a thick stick or bottle filled with water. Although pounding the pulp is historically more authentic than using electric appliances, it is hard work, and time-consuming.

As you make the pulp, pour it into a bucket or large plastic bottle until you have enough for several sheets. Approximately one load in the blender will make one thin sheet of 8½" x 11" paper or a slightly thicker sheet of 5½" x 8½" paper. You will have to experiment to determine which thickness you prefer. If the pulp is too thick, simply add more water, but do not dilute it too much as this will produce fine, fragile sheets which may be difficult to work with until you are more experienced.

Torn strips of paper are soaked in water before being macerated in the blender.

Note: Be careful not to beat the pulp for too long. A good way to test whether the pulp has been beaten enough, is to put a teaspoon of beaten pulp into a jar of water. Seal the lid and shake the jar. If you can see individual fibers floating in the water, the pulp has reached the right consistency. If there are still clumps or whole pieces left, it must be blended a little longer. If the pulp has reached a creamy consistency with no fibers visible, it has been beaten for too long — the fibers will be too short to bond together strongly.

Pouring pulp onto felt

Lay a dry piece of felt onto a wide tray or several sheets of newspaper. Make sure the felt is totally flat and level. Place the frame on the felt, allowing a margin of fabric all around.

Fill a half-gallon jug (or large milk carton) with pulp from the bucket, and with a rapid movement of your wrist, pour the pulp over the felt within the frame. Give the underlying tray or felt a quick shake to the right and left, forwards and backwards. This disperses the fibers evenly and creates a uniform sheet of paper. Stop shaking the tray after the initial dispersion, otherwise the fibers will separate again as the water drains away. Allow the water to drain for about a minute, mopping it up outside the frame with a sponge until most of the water has drained away. Remove the frame carefully, and lay another dry piece of felt on top of the wet sheet. Press the felt down gently with the flat of your hand until it begins to absorb water. Then lay a sponge over the top felt and allow it to absorb the moisture. Wring out the sponge and repeat this process until most of the excess water has been removed. Now roll a rolling pin slowly but firmly over the covering felt — this will not only press the paper, but also remove more water. When you have removed as much excess water as possible, carefully peel the top felt off the lower one, and hang up the sheet of paper, still on the lower felt, to dry.

Pouring paper pulp onto felt inside a frame.

Pressing the wet paper with a rolling pin between two felts.

> *Note: Take care not to press the paper with the rolling pin too soon. If the paper is still very wet, too much pressure with the rolling pin will displace the fibers and you may tear the sheet.*

It is not always necessary to use the same fabric below and above the wet sheet. The top piece can be of any cotton or woolen fabric, but bear in mind that its texture will be impressed on the surface of your paper. Cheesecloth creates a lovely surface texture on which to draw.

Storing leftover pulp

Newly made or leftover pulp can be stored in sealed bottles or buckets for a few weeks. If it starts to smell, add 1 teaspoon of household bleach per each 2 quarts of pulp. Before using the pulp again, however, you must rinse it very thoroughly. Pour it through a drainage bag, stocking or colander lined with mesh, rinse well under running water and return it to a bucket or bottle, slightly diluted. Experience will tell you which consistency works best, but a general rule for the pouring method is to dilute one cup of wet, *drained* pulp with one to two cups of water, depending on the thickness of paper required. If the pulp is too thick, you may get lumpy sheets.

To facilitate storing, you can drain excess pulp through mesh to reduce its bulk and then store it in the refrigerator in a sealed plastic bag. Dilute it as explained above before use. If you want to store pulp indefinitely, drain it through a stocking and hang it up to dry. When you need some, simply break off pieces of the dried material, soak it in water for an hour and blend again.

Pulp can be stored wet or dry.

PROJECT 1
Two sheets of plain paper

REQUIREMENTS
Basic equipment list (see p. 16)
Small embroidery or picture frame
Five facial tissues or three paper napkins
2 cups of boiling water
Four pieces of cotton fabric
Iron and ironing board
Tray

The wet sheet of paper can be ironed dry between two pieces of fabric.

Tear the tissues into strips, place these in a jug and add the boiling water. Leave to stand for about ten minutes. Lay a handkerchief or a piece of cotton fabric on the tray, making sure that the material is flat and the tray level. Position the frame centrally on the fabric. Blend the tissues and water in the blender for five seconds (or beat it with an egg beater) to a creamy pulp. In the meantime, switch on the iron, setting it to medium heat.

Now quickly pour the blended pulp onto the fabric inside the frame and shake the tray to disperse the fibers. Allow the water to drain for about a minute, mopping it up outside the frame with a sponge. Lay the second piece of fabric on top (covering both pulp and frame) and continue mopping until most of the water has drained away. Lift the top layer of fabric and carefully remove the frame. Replace the top piece of fabric and gently roll a rolling pin over the paper 'sandwich.' Then carefully peel off the top piece of fabric and replace it with a dry one. Smooth it down well and begin ironing until the fabric feels dry. Turn the paper 'sandwich' over and peel away the remaining piece of wet fabric. Replace it with dry fabric and iron until it feels dry. Continue ironing on both sides until the paper is bone-dry, and peel off one of the pieces of fabric. Insert a knife under a corner of the paper to lift an edge, turn the paper face down, and peel the other piece of fabric away from it.

PROJECT 2
Two sheets of mottled paper

Mottled paper is made by mixing two different kinds of pulp. Make one cup of colored tissue pulp, and one cup of plain pulp. To prepare the latter, tear wastepaper such as notepaper, envelopes or computer paper into small pieces and add boiling water. Leave to stand for an hour and then macerate in a blender for 20 seconds. Proceed as for Project 1, but pour the plain and colored pulp into the frame simultaneously. As you shake the tray, the pulp will blend together, forming a mottled sheet of paper. Iron dry as before.

Opposite: Equipment and paper from Project 1.

Right: Papers from Projects 1 and 2.

Chapter 3
Making paper with a mould

The mold with its newly formed sheet of paper is left to drain over the vat

Now that you have made your first few sheets of paper, you will have gained some understanding of the properties and possibilities of paper pulp. When broken down and mixed with water, plant fibers will bond together to form paper. (In the case of recycling, the fibers used will usually be those of wood pulp.)

The method of paper-making described in this chapter is the most common, and bears the closest resemblance to the process used both traditionally and in modern industry. The pulp is suspended in water in a container called a vat, in the ratio of 2–5 per cent pulp to 95-98 per cent water. A screen known as a paper-maker's mold is lowered into the vat and lifted out of the pulp. The water drains through the screen and leaves a thin layer of pulp on the mesh. This 'wet sheet' is transferred onto a piece of fabric called a felt and the process repeated until there is a pile of felts which can then be pressed. The felts with their sheets of paper are then removed individually to dry.

The following equipment is needed for this method of paper-making:

The mold

The mold is the most important piece of equipment for the paper-maker. It consists of a simple rectangular frame with mesh stretched across it to form a sieve for the pulp.

The molds of professional paper-makers are usually made with mahogany frames and brass wire mesh, with strong joints above to stand up to years of immersion in water. It is also customary to have two molds to each deckle, which makes it possible for one mold to drain while the other is dipped into the vat containing the pulp. For the amateur it is, however, possible to make paper with simpler and less expensive molds.

Improvised molds

❑ A simple round mold can be made by stretching nylon net curtaining over an embroidery frame.

❑ A flat wire sieve (such as a spatter shield) can also be used to form round sheets.

❑ A picture frame with net curtaining stapled onto it will work well for small sheets. A picture fame of the same size, with the net omitted, can be used as a 'deckle' (see p. 26).

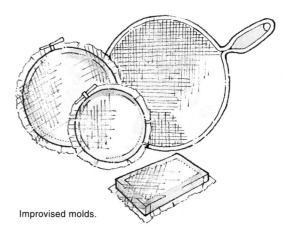

Improvised molds.

The paper-maker's mold

A more durable but simple frame can be made from wood. The inside dimensions of the frame will be determined by the size of the paper you wish to make. The measurements for two frame sizes are given below.

1. To make sheets of 8½" x 11" paper, the inside area of the frame will measure 8½" x 11". Strips of wood for the frame should measure 1" x 2". You will need two pieces 8½ inches long and two pieces 13 inches long, simply glued and nailed together at the corners. The corners can be further reinforced with brass L-shaped braces.

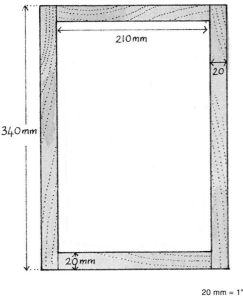

20 mm = 1"
210 mm = 8½"
340 mm = 13"

Dimensions for a mold to make an 8½" x 11" sheet.

2. To make paper approximately 5½" x 8½" in size, the inside dimensions of the frame will be 5½" x 8½". The strips of wood should measure 1" x 1" and you will need two pieces 5½ inches long, and two pieces 10½ inches long.

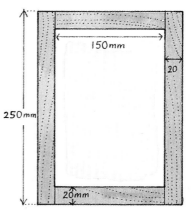

Dimensions for a mold to make a 5½" x 8½" sheet.

20 mm = 1"
150 mm = 5½"
250 mm = 10½"

When the frame is finished, it must be covered with mesh, stretched as taut as possible. The mesh can be pinned or stapled to the frame. Materials that can be used as mesh include net curtaining, fiberglass window screening, plastic cross-stitch fabric, silk-screen mesh, or any porous fabric with a fine gauge. If you use fabric, wet it before stretching, as some kinds tend to sag when placed in water, resulting in sheets of paper of uneven thickness. When making the mold, avoid using ferrous metals, as this will cause foxing and ruin the paper. Foxing is the brownish rust stain which develops when pulp or paper comes into contact with metal objects.

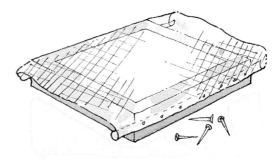

The mesh is stretched taut as it is nailed to the frame

Irregular deckle-edges characteristic of handmade paper

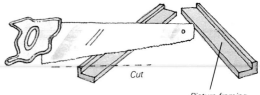

Picture framing

Saw the molding with the help of a mitre box and fasten it at the corners so that it rests quite firmly on the mold. The corners may be reinforced with brass L-shaped branches and the joints glued with woodglue for further strength.

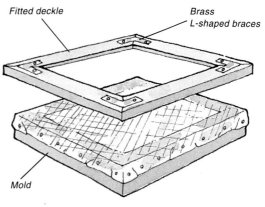

Fitted deckle   Brass L-shaped braces

Mold

The deckle

The deckle, a removable open frame the same size as the mold, rests on top of the mesh and contains the pulp within the surface area of the screen. This determines the size of the sheet of paper to be formed, and causes the irregular deckle-edge so characteristic of handmade paper. Without the deckle, the paper will be thinner and the edge more irregular.

For a simple but perfectly adequate deckle, make a second frame identical to the mold but only 1 inch deep and omit the mesh.

A more sophisticated deckle to fit snugly onto the mold will require a bit of carpentry. It can be constructed from picture frame molding 1½ inch wide, including a flange ¼ inch wide. You will need approximately 5 feet for a deckle to fit an 8½" x 11" mold (this allows for waste during cutting).

The vat

The vat is a large container for holding the water and pulp with which the paper is made. It must be large enough to accommodate the mold and deckle held in both hands. A square plastic dishpan with a capacity of about 5 gallons of water is perfect for making 8½" x 11" sheets, while a square tub (with a capacity of about 3 gallons) will be fine for making smaller sheets of paper. For making larger sheets of paper on a larger mold, you can use a water storage tank, bus box (from restaurant suppliers) or a chemical drum cut in half.

Felt

The wet sheets of paper are transferred from the mold onto absorbent fabric, traditionally felted woolen cloth (see p. 16).

Forming the paper with a mold

A bucket of prepared pulp (about 2 gallons) will make 20 to 25 sheets of thinnish 8½" x 11" paper. You will have to experiment with the thickness you require, but start off by pouring

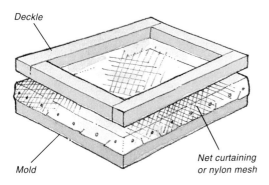

Deckle

Mold   Net curtaining or nylon mesh

3 quarts of pulp into the vat and add cold water up to about 3 inches from the top.

Before you begin, agitate the pulp in the vat by stirring it gently with your hand or a wooden spoon. This must be done before forming each sheet, as the pulp tends to settle on the bottom. Do not stir too wildly, as too much turbulence in the vat will result in paper with lumps and ridges. Dampen the mesh on the mold before forming your first sheet, to facilitate drainage of the pulp.

Facing the vat, hold the mold with both hands by the short sides and lower it vertically into the far side of the vat. Then gently tilt the mold towards you until it is lying horizontally, about 2 inches below the surface of the water. Be careful not to bump the sides of the vat with the mold, as this causes ridges. Gradually lift the mold, holding it level, and allow it to drain over the vat for about 15 seconds, until most of the water has drained away. Then tilt it slightly to drain for another ten seconds. If you have two molds, you could put the one aside to drain while you form another sheet with the other. After every two or three sheets, add another quart of pulp to the vat.

If you are unhappy with a sheet, simply invert the mold and lower it onto the pulp in the vat. When the pulp has fallen from the mold, stir the pulp in the vat well and dip the mold again.

Using a deckle

Hold the deckle against the mold with your thumbs on top and fingers underneath as you immerse both frames in the vat. Lift them out of the vat and as they clear the surface but before the water drains away, give the mold and deckle a gentle shake backwards, forwards and sideways to disperse the fibers. Relax as you do this, moving from the shoulders and not just the wrists. Then drain the wet sheet in the same way as when using a mold. After about 30 seconds you should be able to remove the deckle gently. Be very careful not to let any drops fall on the wet sheet — these will form little spots of thinner pulp, or 'water marks'.

> **Note:** As a general rule, you will need slightly less pulp in the vat when forming sheets with a deckle than without. Start with 2½ quarts and add more as you proceed.

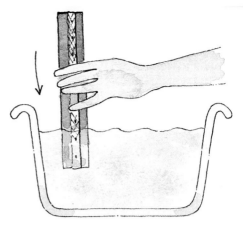

Lower the mold and deckle into the vat

Tilt the mold towards you while it is still submerged under water.

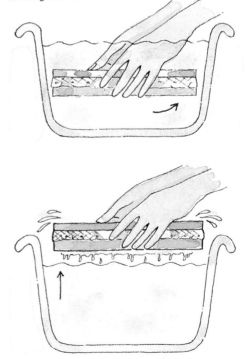

Lift the mold out of the water and give it a shake.

Drying a sheet on the mold

At this point, you can simply tilt the frame on its side and leave it to dry. It will dry much quicker outside in the sun, or next to a heater. On a windy or sunny day, the paper will dry in a couple of hours.

In sunny weather and with two molds in operation, it is possible to make up to 12 sheets a day using this method. Strong winds can, however, topple the mold and ruin the paper. To prevent this, lean the mold against a flower pot in a sunny position with a brick or heavy stone placed at the base to hold it firm. Be careful, too, of rain or garden sprinklers, as any water falling on the wet pulp will displace the fibers and create holes. Furthermore do not leave your paper outside overnight, as slugs and snails will make short work of it. To remove the paper from the mold, slide a sharp knife under a corner of the paper and work it along the top edge to loosen it. Then gently peel off the paper.

The couching method

The term 'couch' probably comes from the French verb *coucher*, meaning 'to lay down'. After forming a wet sheet on a mold and allowing it to drain sufficiently, you can couch it onto a piece of wet felt.

First, create a small pile of about five to six *wet* felts to form a soft pad to facilitate couching. Without this pad, the first few sheets could be formed badly. A wet folded towel or wet piece of carpet pad may also be placed underneath the pad of felts to create a suitable mound. After creating a pile of about ten sheets of paper, the towel or underfelt should be removed—the pile of wet felts and paper will be sufficient.

Rest the mold with the long left-hand side of the frame against the right-hand side of the felt, with the wet paper facing to the left. Hold the mold vertically, so that your left hand holds the raised left side of the frame. Using both hands and a gentle rolling motion, lower the mold (pulp against the felt) down flat on the felt with

The paper can be left on the mold and dried outside in the sun.

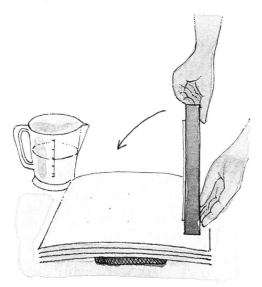

Rest the mold on the right side of the felt, pulp facing left.

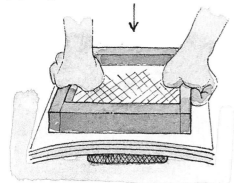

Roll the mold firmly against the felt from right to left in a smooth rocking motion.

Lift the mold on the right, leaving the wet sheet on the felt.

your left hand, and lift it up with the right. While the motion should be smooth, the pressure should be sufficient to transfer the wet pulp onto the felt. Press the mold quite firmly if you are unsure to begin with. With practice you should soon be able to do this in one smooth, fairly rapid movement. Do not be disheartened if the first sheet is not successful, as it often causes problems. Place another wet felt on top of the first sheet of paper, and couch a second sheet onto this. Continue in this manner until you have a substantial pile of felts and paper. The pile should then be pressed.

The professional couching method is to hold up what is known as a post of felts (144 sheets), which is then pressed. For the amateur working at home, a good number is between 20 and 50 sheets. This will, however, be determined by the number of felts you have (*see* Chapter 4 for pressing and drying a post of felts).

It is important to have the correct amount of moisture in the felts. They must be quite damp, but not sopping wet. This comes with practice, but as a general rule for the beginner, they should rather be too wet than too dry.

The couching of pulp from right to left is not a rigid rule and if you are left-handed you may want to try it the other way round. Some people also couch from back to front, rolling the mold toward them. Experiment to find the method you find most comfortable.

> **Note:** It is possible to couch sheets of paper onto nonwoven dressmaker's interfacing, handkerchiefs, pieces of cotton or silk and then iron them dry. Simply wet a piece of thinner fabric of your choice, place it on a wet pile of felts and couch as usual. To iron, follow the method described in Project 1. Bear in mind that the texture of the fabric will be reflected in the texture of the sheet of paper. Thinner fabrics are unsuitable when hanging the paper up to dry as the paper tends to curl badly (or cockle, as it is generally known), particularly in the case of bigger sheets. To keep the paper from curling, remove it from the fabric just before it has dried completely and press it between blotting paper, replacing the blotting paper with dry sheets when it becomes damp. Store the paper in a heavy book for a week.

PROJECT 3
Round sheet of paper, ironed dry

REQUIREMENTS
Small embroidery frame (6-inch in diameter)
with net curtaining stretched across it
Mixing bowl or plastic container large enough
for immersed frame
1 quart of prepared pulp
Iron, ironing board and two handkerchiefs for
ironing

Pour 2 cups of the pulp into the bowl and top it up with water to about 1 inch below the rim. Wet the mesh on the frame by dipping it upside down in the bowl. Holding the frame with both hands on either side with the mesh facing you, lower it vertically into the bowl. Gradually tilt it horizontally towards you, making sure it is well below the surface of the water. Slowly lift the frame, giving it a slow shake in all directions as it reaches the surface. Lift it above the water and allow it to drain for about 20 seconds. Gently remove the net from the frame, cover with a dry handkerchief and iron dry as in Project 1 *see* p. 21), peeling the net from the back of the paper when bone-dry. Leave the rest of the pulp in the bowl for Project 4.

PROJECT 4
Round sheet of paper, air-dried on the frame

Pour the rest of the pulp into the bowl. Using the same embroidery frame, form a wet sheet in the bowl as for Project 3 and allow it to drain for ten seconds. Then, in a warm spot, tilt the frame on its side and allow the paper to dry completely. To remove, simply insert a sharp knife under a corner of the paper, work it around the edge, and peel the paper off the net. Press it in a heavy book for a week.

Opposite: Finished papers from Projects 3 and 4. One sheet is left to dry on the frame.

Right: A round sheet of paper couched onto a wet handkerchief laid over a damp pad.

PROJECT 5
Couching two sheets of paper

REQUIREMENTS
Same as for Project 3, plus
Three handkerchiefs
Towel
Two dishcloths

First make a small pad with a folded towel and two dishcloths and wet them well. Make sure they are well smoothed out, with no bubbles trapped between the layers of fabric. Lay a wet handkerchief on top and smooth down as before. Using the method explained in Project 3, form a sheet of paper on an embroidery frame and couch it onto a handkerchief in a smooth rolling motion. Lay the handkerchief and its wet paper on newspaper for half an hour and then hang it up to dry. Repeat for the second sheet. Remove the paper from the handkerchief before it is completely dry and press it between blotting paper, replacing the blotting paper with dry sheets when it becomes damp. Press the paper in a heavy book for a week.

> **Note:** *You can also use a small picture frame with net curtain stapled onto it, or if you already have a 5½" x 8½" mold, you can pour 1 quart of pulp into a kitchen sink, top it up with water, and form and couch two sheets of paper as described above.*

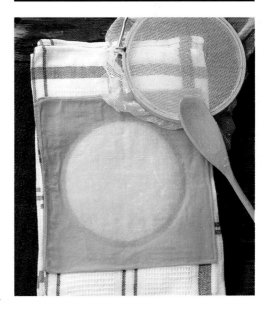

Chapter 4
Pressing and drying paper

Various pressing methods

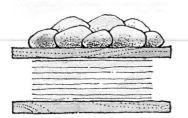

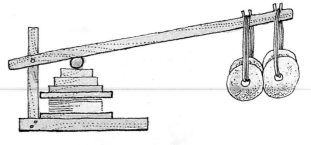

Early pressing method

Simple pressing method

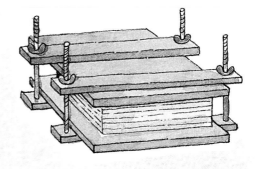

Simple screw press

Simple pressing method

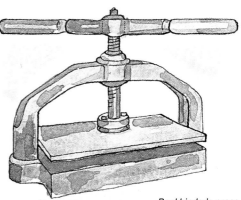

Bookbinder's press

Pressing is necessary both before and after drying sheets of paper. The purpose of pressing a post of wet sheets on felt is to bond the fibers firmly and remove as much excess water as possible before separating the felts for drying. This also speeds up the drying process and prevents the paper from curling or cockling. Pressing the dry paper will flatten and smooth it.

Early pressing methods in the East were simple, employing pressing boards and heavy rocks piled on top of the post, or a simple lever press with weights hung on the end of a pole. Pressure was gradually increased over several hours. Western paper-makers, on the other hand, traditionally pressed their post of felts in wooden screw presses tightened by means of a long wooden lever. Today Western mills making handmade paper use powerful hydraulic presses which can exert a pressure of between 100 and 150 tons. Although most Japanese paper-makers today also use screw or hydraulic presses, the emphasis still falls on gradually applying pressure rather than rapidly as is the case in the West. This is worth bearing in mind when making paper from plants.

Pressing paper

The simplest method of pressing a pile of felts is to sandwich it between two boards and to stand on it for ten minutes. The heavier you are, the more effective the method. To continue the pressure, stack bricks on the board and leave it for a couple of hours. Alternatively, place a large bucket on top and fill it with water or sand.

A simple press can be made with two pieces of hardwood (or varnished pine to avoid warping) larger than the felts, clamped with four strips of wood and carriage bolts.

Once you have a post of felts, transfer it to the press and screw down the carriage bolts. If you turn the press on its side and leave it to stand vertically on a sink or draining board, it takes about half an hour for most of the excess water to drain. You can then separate the felts for drying.

If you are lucky enough to get hold of a bookbinder's press, it will be perfect for pressing paper. Simply slide in the felts (sandwiched between boards) and screw down the press until you have applied a fair amount of pressure. After about 10 minutes, give the lever another turn to increase the pressure. Leave the pile in the press for about half an hour before removing it.

Separating the felts

After opening the press, peel away the top felt to reveal the first wet sheet of paper. Each felt with its wet sheet must be separated from the one below and dried individually. To separate the felts, peel them apart carefully, gently lifting a corner without lifting the sheet below. If the sheet below begins lifting, lower the felt and try another edge. This process cannot be hurried.

Drying the paper

It is advisable to dry couched paper indoors, away from wind, sun or rain. If it dries too quickly or unevenly, the edges will cockle. Felts can be hung from a drying rack or clothesline with clothespins. Newspapers can be used to catch the drips.

Alternatively you can lay the individual felts down flat on newspaper, although this takes up a lot of space. It is also preferable to let the air circulate around the felts. In warm weather and dry climates, the paper should be dry in one or two days. In winter it will take longer. To speed up the drying process, lay the wet sheets (on their felts) down flat on sheets of newspaper for a few hours prior to hanging them up. When the felts feel dry to the touch, the sheets of paper can be removed.

Removing the paper from the felt

To remove the dry paper from the felt, first slide a sharp knife under a corner of the paper and work the knife along the top edge to loosen it. Then turn the felt over so that the paper is face down (on a clean, dry surface) and gently peel the felt away from the paper. When the felts have been used for some time, this process becomes easier. At first, you may have to work the knife around the entire edge of the paper until it comes away cleanly.

Once you have removed the paper from the felts, press them in a heavy book for a week. Alternatively, interleave them with stiff cardboard and press them between pressing boards weighted down with bricks. If you have a screw or hydraulic press, 24 hours of pressure should be sufficient. As the paper is still unsized (i.e., no substance has been added to it to make it less absorbent) you can at this stage write on the paper only with ballpoint or pencil, not ink.

Couched paper on felts hanging up to dry

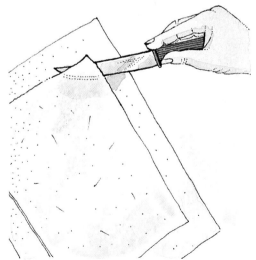

Removing dried paper from felt with a knife

How to make a 'weight brick'

A useful piece of equipment for both the hand-papermaker and the bookbinder is a weight brick. Find a smooth brick and wrap it (like a parcel) with two sheets of newspaper. Secure the newspaper tightly with adhesive tape, and then cover the whole with a layer of colored or decorative paper. To press your (dry) paper, cards, envelopes or book, stack them between two boards and place the brick on top.

Wrap a brick tightly in two layers of newspaper.

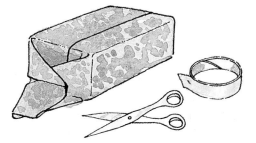

Wrap the covered brick with decorative paper.

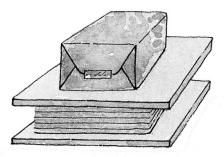

Press dry paper between boards under the brick.

Opposite: Wet sheets on their felts, laid on newspapers to dry.

Above right: A post of felts and paper, couched one on top of the other.

PROJECT 6
Couching a post of ten sheets of 8½" x 11" paper

For this project you will need to invest in a few items of equipment and make a larger quantity of pulp than previously.

REQUIREMENTS
Basic equipment (see p. 16)
15 felts
8½" x 11" mold
6 quarts of white pulp

To tint the pulp slightly, make a pot of tea and add the liquid to the pulp in the bucket. Stir it in well and leave the pulp to stand for an hour. Then pour 3 quarts of prepared pulp into the vat and top up with water. Using a mold without a deckle, form ten sheets of paper and couch them onto wet felts, one on top of the other, until you have a post (*see* pp. 28-29 for instructions on couching). Remember to add 1 quart of pulp to the tub after every two to three sheets. Press the post, using one of the methods described above, before separating the felts and hanging them up to dry. When dry, remove the sheets from the felts and press them under weights or in a heavy book for a week.

The
healing comes
when we
stop fighting
the condition

JOEL GOLDSMITH

Faye Collins
12 Denver Place
2040 Honeydew.

Dear Letta

...on for the beautiful photograph
...urself — I will treasure it. It will
...e good in a brass frame ...possibly
...cked with home-made paper.
...r own sheets are almost dry now
...and will be put in the press for 24
hours to flatten them, and thereafter
will be stored under weights for a
week or two. I have sized them, so
you will be able to write on them

— Have fun. and lots of love

Marianne

Rosebank 7700

7700

14 Febru...

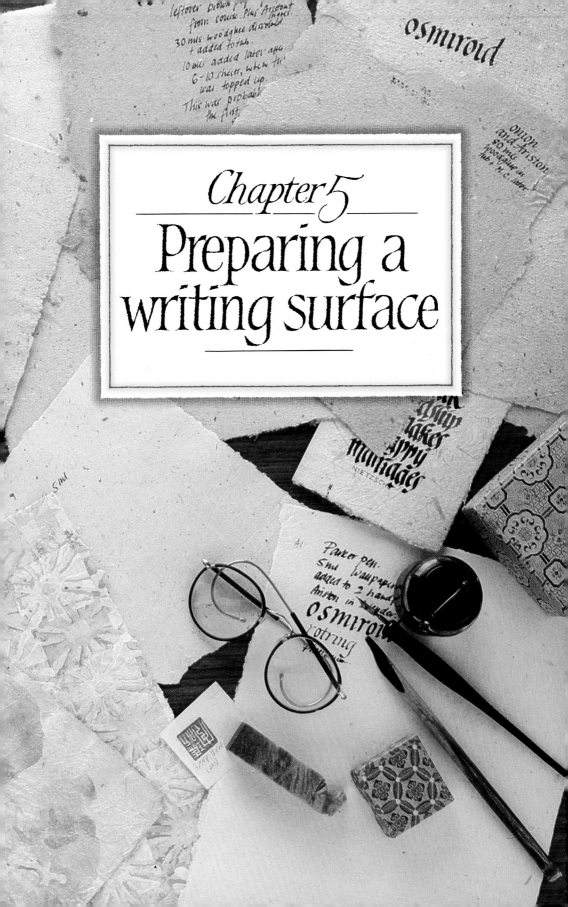

Chapter 5
Preparing a writing surface

In order to be able to write on paper with ink, the paper must be sized, that is, a glue-like substance must be added to the paper to render it less absorbent. Sizing also strengthens paper. Unsized paper is good for printing, including linoleum block printing, and you can write on it with ballpoint or pencil, but you can not use calligraphy inks. If the paper is unsized, the ink will bleed, as it does when you write on blotting paper or tissue. Papers in the East are traditionally unsized because wood blocks were originally used for printing and only one side of the paper was used. Western printing methods, however, demanded a well-sized opaque paper, suitable for printing on both sides without showing through. Gelatine sizing was traditionally used before being replaced by chemical methods of sizing.

The following sizing methods are simple and the ingredients available in most supermarkets. The methods either entail sizing the paper after it has dried, or adding a sizing substance to pulp in a vat. All quantities given for the latter apply to a bucket of prepared pulp (about 2 gallons). Approximate measurements are given, as a handful of soaked paper used to make one load of pulp in a blender varies from person to person. The quantity of size will alter accordingly and minor adjustments may have to be made to suit your needs. It is always advisable to write down all your experiments in a notebook so that you can repeat successful ones and adjust unsuccessful ones. You are encouraged to experiment and find the method that gives you the best results for your requirements.

Gelatine sizing is historically one of the most popular methods in the West because of its inherent stability and neutral pH. It also produces an excellent surface for calligraphy inks. Dissolve 1 heaping teaspoon of gelatine in 1 cup of boiling water, and use a wide, soft paintbrush to paint it onto dry paper still on its felt. After sizing the paper, hang it up again to dry. Sizing it twice with less concentrated gelatine (approximately ½ teaspoon to 1 cup water) is sometimes better than one sizing, as there will be less risk of streaking or bubbling.

The above quantity will size about ten sheets. Mixing more is impractical, as the gelatine begins to cool and set after a few sheets. The disadvantage of this method is that the gelatine has to be hot, and the sizing can only be done

after the paper has dried. Also, the paper will be more effectively sized on one side than the other.

Use a soft paintbrush to size the paper with a gelatine solution

Note: Paper must not be too acidic or alkaline. If acids are present, the molecular structure of the cellulose in the paper breaks down, causing it to become discolored, weak and brittle. Alkalinity and acidity can be conveniently measured with a pH indicator (a type of litmus paper) and the scale ranges from 14 (extremely alkaline) to 1 (extremely acid). Red wine, for example, has a pH of about 3½ while milk has a pH of between 6 and 7. A pH of 7 is regarded as neutral. However, exposure to the atmosphere renders any paper acidic over time, so a pH of about 8 is regarded as safer by conservationists. For this reason, it is best to avoid sizing methods that increase the acidity of the paper, such as the rosin and alum sizing frequently used by large paper-mills.

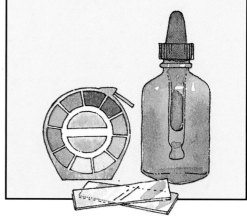

Fels Naptha soap makes a good size. Grate about ¾ ounce (use a postal scale) of soap and dissolve it in 1 quart of boiling water. When cool, it sets into a jelly, which is then further diluted in boiling water. Add this to the pulp in a bucket, stirring it in well. Couch or air-dry the paper as explained previously. It forms a beautiful surface to write on, but for long-lasting papers the pH might be suspect.

Starch can be used on its own, or in conjunction with another sizing method such as gelatine. Dissolve 4 teaspoons in a little cold water, stir it into a jug of boiling water until it thickens and add it to the pulp in a bucket (about 2 gallons). It produces paper with a pleasant surface to write on and when you shake the sheet, you will hear a firm rattling sound. For calligraphy inks the paper will need further sizing (¾ teaspoon of gelatine in 1 cup of boiling water, painted on with a soft watercolor brush). Increasing the amount of starch in order to size the paper in one operation is not successful, as the pulp thickens and becomes less manageable in the vat. The water also takes longer to drain through the mesh.

Carpenter's glue (4 teaspoons of glue dissolved in a jug of boiling water) can be added to the pulp in a bucket. For calligraphy inks a second sizing with gelatine (¾ teaspoon of gelatine dissolved in 1 cup of boiling water) will improve the surface. Carpenter's glue produces paper with a good writing surface and a firm rattling sound when shaken, but the pH is suspect.

Methyl cellulose (low substitution powder) can be obtained from arts and crafts suppliers in amounts of 4 ounces. Although this method of sizing is expensive and not as readily available as those listed above, it is excellent because of its stability and neutral pH. It must be made up at least 24 hours before use, as it takes a while to dissolve.

Dissolve 1 tablespoonful in a little water until it forms a thick jelly, then gradually dilute it until you have 2 quarts of solution. Methyl cellulose is convenient because it has a long shelf life and can be sprayed onto dry paper with a small spray gun, producing an excellent surface for calligraphy. A good drenching — the paper may be quite wet after spraying — will ensure that the paper is well sized.

Spraying a solution of methyl cellulose onto paper in order to size it.

PROJECT 7
Sizing tinted paper in two operations

REQUIREMENTS
Basic equipment (see p. 16)
8½" x 11" mold and deckle
6 quarts of prepared pulp
Household starch
Gelatine
Wide, soft paintbrush
Two sheets of brightly colored paper

Shred two sheets of colored paper and pour boiling water over the shreds. Leave to stand for 15 minutes and then blend small handfuls for seven seconds at a time. Add this mixture to the 6 quarts of pulp.

Dissolve 3 teaspoons of household starch in a little cold water, stir in boiling water until it thickens and add it to the pulp. Mix well and leave to stand for an hour. Pour 2½ quarts of the pulp-and-starch mixture into a vat, topping up with water. Using a mold and deckle, form and couch ten sheets of paper in the usual manner. Press the post and hang the felts up to dry.

To size the dry sheets still on their felts, dissolve ¾ teaspoon of gelatine in 1 cup of boiling water, stirring well until all gelatine globules have dissolved. Use a wide, soft brush to paint on the gelatine solution from left to right. Hang up the sheets of paper to dry — this should take about 24 hours. Remove the sheets from the felts and press them in a heavy book for a week or two. Alternatively, stack them between sheets of ordinary cardboard and place them under a board and weights for a week.

Chapter 6
Colouring and texturing paper

Coloring handmade paper can create beautiful effects in a range of colors. A simple method is to blend colored paper and add it to the pulp. Alternatively, various natural and chemical dyes can be added to the pulp, creating subtle tints and shades of paper. The addition of textural interest in the form of petals, leaves, fabric oddments or cotton thread further enhances the handmade sheet. This chapter includes a variety of different coloring and texturing methods.

Coloring the paper

Colored, crepe, or tissue paper can be torn up and soaked for a few hours. Add a few pieces of these to the blender when you blend the other pulp. Black paper can be added to create darker shades.

Natural dyes can be derived from tea or coffee or the liquids of boiled plant fibers, such as onion skins, berberis, bark, beets, privet or wandering jew, or powdered spices, such as turmeric or ginger. Blend the pulp with the liquid or spice to mix it in well.

Powdered paint, inks or food coloring can be added in small quantities to the pulp in a blender. If you add ½ teaspoon per blender load it will result in a pale tint, whereas 1 teaspoon will create quite an intense color.

Simple dyes, for example Dylon, batik or Dr. Martin's dyes are obtainable from hobby and art shops. Mixed according to the instructions and added to the pulp in a bucket, these dyes result in attractive colors. It is best to leave most dyes in the pulp for an hour or two before making the paper.

Textile pigments or dyes are sold in large quantities — the smallest are usually 2- or 10-lb. tubs — and they are usually quite expensive. However, they go a long way, so if you need large quantities of dye, the basic textile dyes, either in powder or liquid form, are excellent. Add them to the pulp in a bucket but use them in minute quantities. Depending on the tint required, ½ teaspoon of powdered paint will color one sheet only, whereas the same quantity of textile pigments will color a whole bucket of pulp.

Natural ingredients can add texture and color.

Texturing the paper

❑ Herbs, pine needles, feathers, pieces of cotton fabric and wool and gold sewing thread can be cut into pieces and added to the pulp in a vat to cause random patterns and textures.
❑ Autumn leaves and flower heads can be boiled for 30 minutes, partially blended and added to the pulp in a vat. Be careful not to overdo it. A little added at a time will be more attractive than too much, and the paper will also be easier to write on.
❑ White or colored paper, only partially blended, can be added to the pulp to create textural interest.
❑ Dried, pressed flowers and herbs, or ferns, feathers and crushed shells can be positioned on a wet sheet. Once pressed, this will form an embossed shape which will remain on the dry paper. Alternatively, a second sheet can be laminated on top of the first sheet to sandwich the objects in between (*see* Chapter 9 for laminating and embossing).
❑ Plant fibers can be prepared according to the instructions in Chapter 7 and added to pulp made by recycling paper.

PROJECT 8
Sizing textured paper in one operation

REQUIREMENTS
Basic equipment (see p. 16)
6 quarts of prepared pulp
Fels Naptha soap
Grater
Powdered paint

Add three teaspoons of red, yellow or blue powdered paint to each load of pulp in the blender. Pour the pulp into a bucket. Then collect two handfuls of flowers or dried autumn leaves and boil them for 30 minutes. Place the cooked plants in the blender with three cups of water and blend for five seconds.

You may need to do this in two batches. Add this to the pulp in the bucket.

Grate about ¾ ounce of Fels Naptha soap and dissolve it in 1 quart of boiling water. When cool, dilute it further with boiling water and add it to the pulp. Stir the soap into the pulp with a wooden spoon, mixing it well. Allow to stand for 30 minutes.

Place 2 quarts of pulp in a vat. Use a mold and deckle to form 15-20 sheets and couch them as usual. Add more pulp after every two sheets. Press the post of sheets and hang the felts up to dry. When dry, the paper should be sized well enough to take most calligraphy inks. Press the sheets in a heavy book or under weights for at least a week before using them.

Materials and finished papers from Project 8.

Chapter 7
Making paper from plants

Paper made from plants has a textural quality that is visually and sensuously beautiful. The smell of some plants lingers in the paper long after it has been made, reminiscent of gardens and meadows in the heat of summer. Fine plant paper resembles Japanese paper in its translucency and strength and feels quite different from paper made by recycling. Even adding plant fibers to recycled paper will enhance its attractiveness and durability. The pleasure of looking for suitable plant materials and processing them for paper-making can lead to an increased interest in botany, ecology and chemistry. Each plant species will respond differently according to the time it is picked, the season, its growing conditions and the method of processing. The sensitive handling of plant fibers becomes important when one attempts to create fine quality paper. As you become familiar with the different plants, you will begin to appreciate the exquisite workmanship of Japanese paper-makers in making their fine, tissue-like but strong and long-lasting papers.

Almost any plant can be used to make paper, but those with long fibers are most successful. Examples of such plants include leeks, celery, spinach, gladioli, irises, day lilies, river reeds, pampas grasses, bamboo leaves, banana plants (stems and leaves), papyrus, cornhusks, red hot pokers, and the Swiss cheese plant.

A pioneer in experiments with vegetable papers

About 200 years ago, when researchers were hunting for an economical alternative to linen and cotton fiber in the mass production of paper, a German naturalist, Dr. Jacob Christian Schaffer, experimented with a variety of vegetable fibers, and published the results of his findings. His six-volume treatise includes paper samples made from potatoes, grape vines, tree moss, cabbage stalks, hemp, straw, reeds, wasps' nests, thistles and oak leaves, among others. Most of the samples include about one–fifth cotton pulp to help bind the fibers together.

The plants were first chopped by hand or beaten by means of a homemade, hand-operated stamping machine. Tough fibers were sometimes first soaked in a stiff lime paste in order to reduce the beating time.

In order to remove some of the substances contained in vegetable fibers that are harmful to paper-making, the plant material must be broken down through decomposition in water.

This is a longer process than that used for recycling paper, but well worth the effort. For the purposes of this book, this is achieved by one of the following methods.

1. Boiling the plant material in plain water for an hour or more.
2. Leaving it to rot or ferment for a few weeks and then boiling it in water.
3. Boiling it in an alkaline solution.
4. Soaking it in an alkaline solution before boiling.

Preparing plant material

Collect a bucket of plant material and cut the material into 1- to 2-inch lengths, using garden shears or a compost shredder. Make a note of the dry weight so that you can repeat successful experiments. Tough material can first be hammered with a mallet.

Checking the dry weight of chopped plants.

Boiling plants in water

Some common vegetables and flowers, or parts thereof, such as celery, leeks, rhubarb, carrot tops, spinach stalks or cauliflower leaves can be boiled for one to three hours: the tougher the plant, the longer the boiling period. Soaking the plants for an hour or two usually reduces the boiling time.

Once boiled, rinse the plants well through a net drainage bag or stocking. Squeeze the contents of the bag to loosen the soft plant material and keep rinsing until the water runs off clear. Then blend small handfuls of plant fibers in a blender in the same way as recycled paper. The time varies according to the toughness of the fiber — some plants will need up to a minute of blending. To save your blender, blend for 20 seconds, pause and then blend again.

Soaking or rotting plants to break down the fibers

As a general rule, soaking tougher plants for a minimum of 24 hours before boiling them will hasten the decomposition and later reduce the time needed for boiling and beating. Banana stems, river reeds or bamboo, for example, will have to be soaked for several weeks or even months. For long soaking periods, put your chopped plants into a bucket, cover them with water and seal the bucket with plastic and preferably also a lid to prevent insects from breeding in the bucket. Leave the bucket in a warm place such as a warm balcony or sunny courtyard for as long as necessary.

Some material such as mown grass can simply be hosed down in a plastic bag or bucket and then left to stand for a few months. Wet it occasionally to speed up the decaying process. Once it has reduced to about a fifth of its original volume and has become slimy and well decomposed, it can be rinsed and boiled. Boil rotted plants outside, as the smell can be quite unpleasant. Boiling grass, for example, resembles the smell in a stable and rapidly attracts flies. I use a hot plate with an extension cord for boiling rotted plants outside.

Boiling plants in alkaline solutions

Japanese paper-makers traditionally boiled plant fibers in a potash solution made by passing water through the ashes of reeds, hardwoods, rice, straw or buckwheat husks. Contemporary Japanese paper-makers use soda ash and occasionally lime or caustic soda for boiling plant fibers. Alkalis, and particularly caustic soda, must be handled with great care.

Soda ash (Sodium carbonate)

Boiling with soda ash is the method preferred by Japanese paper-makers, who stress the gentle processing of plant fibers and avoid caustic soda which can cause damage. Soda ash is easy and fairly safe to work with. It is not necessary to wear gloves or worry excessively about spillage and mess as is the case with caustic soda. Soda ash is also cheaper, but you may need to order it through your drugstore.

Boil plants in soda ash in the ratio of 20 per cent ash to the dry weight of the plant material. A 5-ounce sample will therefore be boiled with 1 ounce of soda ash (about 3 tablespoons), in 2 quarts of water. Boil for four to five hours, stirring and turning the plants every half hour. To check whether the material is ready, pull the fibers apart, with and against the grain. If ready, they should separate easily. For experiments with tougher plants, increase the boiling time and amount of soda ash before you try caustic soda.

Leave the pot to cool before rinsing, then drain the contents through a net drainage bag, immersing the bag repeatedly in fresh buckets of water until the water runs off clear. Squeeze the bag regularly to loosen the soft plant material, leaving the fibers suitable for paper-making. Once clean, the plants can be blended into pulp and couched as usual.

Before blending, you could beat the fibers by hand for five minutes to reduce the time needed for blending, which weakens the fibers. I put drained boiled plants into a bucket and pound it with the flat end of an axe handle. In the case of some plants (e.g., papyrus), hand-beating, which results in stronger paper, may be all that is necessary. I drain the fibers and beat them on a board with the flat edge of a heavy strip of wood for 10-20 minutes.

Hand-beating cooked papyrus fibers on a board.

Caustic soda or lye (Sodium hydroxide)

Caustic soda must be treated with caution. Although the chemical is very effective in breaking down quite tough plant material, it is highly toxic to plants and animals and has a corrosive effect on most metals. It is advisable to use a stainless steel pot and to boil the plants on a hot plate somewhere out of the way. If the pot boils over, the caustic soda will ultimately eat away the enamel surface of the stove. Do not boil the plants in an aluminum pot or pressure cooker. Aluminum reacts with alkalis, and when it comes into contact with caustic soda, it gives off toxic fumes and will corrode almost immediately. I know of paper-makers who have used aluminum pots with disastrous results: the caustic soda burned a hole in the pot, their plant material was all over the floor and they also had to put up with the oppressive smell of burnt fiber and caustic soda. Other paper-makers I know have reported massive explosions while using pressure cookers to boil

A variety of papers made from papyrus.

Boiling plants outside on a small one-plate stove.

plants in caustic soda.

When mixing caustic soda with water, bring the water to just under boiling point and *then* add the caustic soda. Stand back, as the caustic soda heats the water, which may bubble violently and spatter if it is too hot. Stir the solution well until the caustic soda has dissolved and only then add the plant fibers. Bring to the boil and reduce the heat to a simmer. Stir and turn the plant material in the solution every half hour, being careful not to inhale the fumes. Drain the plant material in an outside drain away from plants or pets and wear rubber gloves for protection.

The amounts of caustic soda used by papermakers vary considerably. Taking 7 ounces of dry plant material and 3 quarts of water as the basic measure, the amount varies between ¾ and 1½ ounces of caustic soda, boiled for one to six hours, depending on the toughness of the material. As a rule of thumb, it is best to use less caustic soda and to increase the boiling time rather than the other way around. Start off with ¾ ounce (about 5 teaspoons), boil the plants for two hours and check whether the fibers are ready. If the plant material still looks green and substantially intact, boil for another two hours. Test and repeat if necessary.

Once boiled, the contents of the pot should resemble the green slime on a stagnant pond. Allow to cool, and rinse well until the water runs off more or less clear.

Soaking plants in an alkaline solution
Soaking in an alkaline solution can reduce prolonged boiling, and on occasion replace boiling altogether. The alkaline soaking method was used by the Chinese to prepare bamboo fibers prior to stamping.

One method is to presoak the fibers in a solution of ¾–1 ounce of caustic soda per quart of water. Place the chopped plants in a bucket and cover them with water. Mix the proportionate amount of caustic soda with a little cold water and add to the plant material in the bucket, stirring well. Cover the bucket with plastic as well as a lid and leave it in a warm place for three to six weeks, stirring daily. Then rinse the fibers well and boil them in water for two to four hours.

A safer method is to soak the plant material for a month in a solution of 1–2 ounces lime (calcium hydroxide) to a quart of water, stirring daily. Then rinse the fibers well and boil for two to four hours.

Bleaching the pulp
Pulp made from plants boiled in caustic soda or soda ash rarely needs further bleaching. The natural shades are attractive and unique to the individual plants. Excessive bleaching can harm the fibers and alter the pH of the paper and is therefore best avoided. However, after boiling, fresh plants tend to retain their green color, and you may want to whiten the pulp. Add 2 tablespoons of household bleach to a bucket of blended pulp and let it stand for an hour or two, stirring occasionally. Then rinse the pulp thoroughly to remove the bleach. If you want to save the bleach, drain the pulp before rinsing it.

> **Note:** *Big hand-paper mills and serious papermakers use large, expensive Hollander beaters for breaking down cotton pulp. A Hollander looks like a large bathtub with a revolving mill wheel on one side which crushes, tears and bruises the cotton pulp against a metal bedplate as it circulates around the 'tub'. This is just not practical for the amateur at home, and the process of breaking down cotton sufficiently into suitable pulp for paper-making using simple kitchen equipment is both time-consuming and beset with difficulties. An alternative is to invent some sort of motor-driven stamping mill, which was historically one of the first successful methods used to break down cotton in Europe. Today stampers are still used in the East for breaking down fibers for Japanese paper-making.*
>
> *An important point is that the kitchen blender is not ideal as a beater, as it cuts the fibers short rather than tearing or bruising them to expose the cellulose.*

How to use a deckle-box

A deckle-box is a useful piece of equipment for making single test sheets without having to blend large quantities of pulp. This is particularly useful when you have a limited amount of pulp, or need to test whether plant fibers have been sufficiently boiled. The deckle-box is similar to the deckle in that it fits on the mold exactly, but its sides are at least 4 inches high. To use the deckle-box, first float the mold in a tub of clean water, and carefully place the deckle-box over it, with the sides fitting flush. Grasp the mold and deckle-box with both hands and push it under the water quickly to remove the air bubbles. Then beat two blender loads of plant fibers, pour the pulp into the inch or so of water inside the deckle-box and stir the pulp. When the pulp has been evenly dispersed, lift the mold and deckle-box out of the water and leave to drain. The sheet can then be couched onto wet felt or a board.

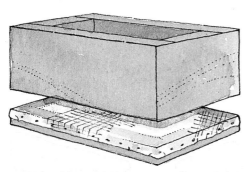

The deckle-box fits the mold exactly.

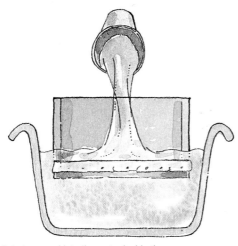

Pulp is poured into the water inside the floating deckle-box.

Note: Traditionally, Western paper was made from used linen or cotton rags, until replaced by wood pulp, which was the more plentiful and economical. Cotton has long fibers (about ⅛ inch long), a high cellulose content (about 90 per cent) and makes very good paper. Together with other plant pulps such as abaca, sisal and flax, cotton is today commercially available in the form of dry compressed boards of prepared pulp (see List of Suppliers at the back of the book).

You can, however, make your own paper from old cotton or linen cloth. Boil torn rags in 2 quarts of water and 2 ounces of caustic soda for 6-8 hours. Then rinse the fabric thoroughly and blend small quantities with at least three cups of water in three bursts of 20 seconds each.

Adding even a small amount of cotton to any paper will improve the quality, making it stronger, more durable and resistant to the effects of aging. If you find processing cotton too lengthy a task, you could recycle mounting-board, watercolor paper, coffee filters, photographic blotters or blotting paper and add the pulp to the plant fibers. However, bear in mind that blending cuts the fibers of recycled cotton paper and shortens them.

Couching onto a board

An alternative method to couching onto felt is to couch the paper directly onto a wooden board. Using this method you will have a dry, flat sheet in a couple of hours. It is not as difficult as it sounds. Once the mold has drained well, turn it face down onto a smooth wooden board and mop up the excess water from the underside of the mesh (the part that is now uppermost) until you can feel the paper is barely damp. Then lift the mold, revealing the paper adhering cleanly to the wooden surface. The board and paper can now be left to dry. In the case of some fibers (such as papyrus or iris) it is possible to dry these sheets in the sun, but high-shrinkage pulps (such as leeks or spinach) tend to curl off the board in strong heat. To be on the safe side, dry the paper indoors if you are unsure of its properties.

Opposite: Plant papers from top to bottom: spinach, pineapple tops, rotted grass, sisal, bamboo and dyed flower petals, unbeaten papyrus, river reed and banana leaves.

From left to right: leek, siberian iris, celery, cornhusk, papyrus, banana leaf, river reed and day lily.

Plants suitable for paper-making

Suitable plants include the leaves and stems of various long-fiberd plants. Some of these involve time-consuming stripping of bark or lengthy beating with sophisticated equipment and are beyond the scope of this book. Listed below is a broad selection of plants which provide good paper-making fibers that can be processed at home by boiling in either soda ash or caustic soda, and beating by hand or with a kitchen blender. In some cases, the tough outer part of the stem or leaves will have to be scraped or peeled before cooking and beating.

Common name	Botanical name	Strip or scrape outer skin	Blend	Handbeat
Bamboo	*Phyllostachys aurea*		✓	
Banana	*Musa nana*		✓	
Canna lily	*Canna indica*	✓	✓	
Common reed	*Phragmites communis*		✓	
Cattail	*Typha latifolia*		✓	
Iris	*Iris*	✓	✓	
Job's tears	*Coix lachruma*			✓
Corn stalks and husks	*Zea mays*		✓	
Mother-in-law's tongue	*Sansevieria trifasciata*	✓	✓	
New Zealand flax	*Phormium tenax*	✓	✓	
Pampas grass	*Cortaderia selloana*		✓	
Papyrus	*Cyperus papyrus*		✓	✓
Pineapple	*Ananas comosus*	✓	✓	
Sisal	*Agave sisalana*	✓	✓	
Bird-of-Paradise	*Strelitzia nicolai*		✓	
Sugar-cane	*Saccharum officinarum*		✓	
Swiss cheese plant	*Monstera deliciosa*		✓	
Wheat straw	*Triticum aestivum*		✓	
Yucca	*Yucca filamentosa*	✓	✓	

PROJECT 9
Ten sheets of onion-skin paper

REQUIREMENTS
5 quarts of prepared plain pulp
Four to six handfuls of onion skins
Starch

Soak the onion skins for an hour and then boil them for three hours. Allow to cool and blend as usual, using the water the onion skins were boiled in. Then add the onion pulp to the prepared pulp in a bucket. Mix 2½ teaspoons of household starch in a little cold water, add to the pulp and stir well. Leave to stand for an hour, stirring occasionally. Pour 2 quarts of pulp into a vat, form and couch the sheets as usual and hang the felts up to dry. When dry, size the paper with gelatine if you want to write on it with calligraphy ink.

PROJECT 10
Cornhusk paper

REQUIREMENTS
9 ounces cornhusks
4½ quarts of water
Cast-iron, enamel or stainless steel pot (mini-
mum capacity 6 quarts)
1¾ ounces soda ash (about 4 tablespoons)

Chop up the cornhusks into pieces about 1 inch long and soak them in a covered bucket which is situated in a warm place for one week. Rinse the cornhusks well and then boil them very gently in soda ash and water for five hours, stirring occasionally. Leave the pot to stand until the pulp is cool and then rinse it thoroughly. Follow the usual procedure for beating and forming the pulp into paper and size if required.

Cornhusk and onion-skin papers.

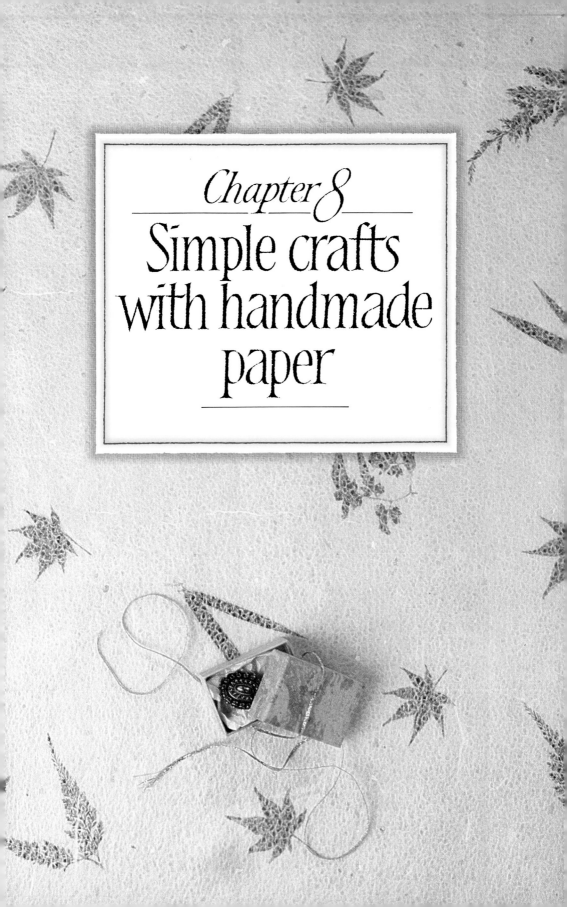

Chapter 8
Simple crafts with handmade paper

Once you have accumulated a variety of sheets of handmade paper, you may want to use them in creative ways as gifts for family or friends. A letter written on handmade paper and sent in a matching envelope is an object of beauty that can be treasured for years, and a pack of ten sheets of paper with matching envelopes is a beautiful gift. By folding handmade paper you can create original cards for special occasions such as christenings, weddings or Valentine's day. In addition, interesting bags, boxes and other containers for gifts can be made from textured handmade paper. The charm of these containers is that no two will be alike.

For most of the crafts in the following two chapters, a few basic items of equipment will be needed.

Bone folder (a bookbinder's tool)
Hobby or craft knife
Steel ruler
Thick cardboard for cutting on
Set square
Pencil
Glue
Scissors
Double-sided tape

Notepaper and cards with matching envelopes.

Notepaper and envelopes

Envelopes are made in exactly the same way as sheets of paper, using a mold and deckle and couching as explained in Chapter 3. Part of the mesh is, however, masked out with a stencil to form an envelope-shaped screen. You may either copy an attractive existing envelope, or follow the instructions for a standard-sized envelope below.

REQUIREMENTS
Stiff cardboard, 13½" x 10"
Carpenter's glue or varnish as a sealer
Paintbrush

Draw the envelope shape on stiff cardboard and cut along the pencil lines with a hobby knife. Leaving a margin of about ¼ inch, remove the inside area and create an 'envelope stencil'. Seal the stencil with two coats of carpenter's glue or varnish to prevent it from disintegrating after a few immersions in water.

To make the envelope, sandwich the stencil firmly between the mold and deckle and lift the pulp onto the mold as usual. After draining the mold for about 30 seconds, lift the deckle a fraction to allow the water lying on the stencil to drain off. Gently wiggle the envelope stencil with one hand to release the fibers overlapping its edges and lift it off the mesh. Be careful not to allow water to drip onto the mold and spoil the paper. Couch the envelope, following the same methods as for paper. Press and dry the envelopes and size them if you want to write on them with ink. Sizing will also strengthen them, which will be useful if you intend sending the envelopes by mail. To fold them, simply fold in the side and bottom flaps and glue them down. Keep the original envelope or diagram as a guide to folding. Graph paper is also useful as a guide for accurate folding.

> **Note:** *Do not try to cut through thick cardboard in one try. Firm pressure with the knife held at a 30-degree angle, and two or three cuts, will result in a cleaner edge. If your arms get tired, you are pressing too hard.*

The stencil can also be made of stiff acetate such as that used for overhead transparencies or X-rays. Acetate has the added advantage of being completely water-resistant.

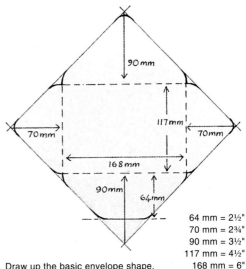

64 mm = 2½"
70 mm = 2¾"
90 mm = 3½"
117 mm = 4½"
168 mm = 6"

Draw up the basic envelope shape.

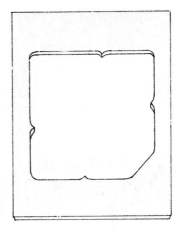

Cut the shape out of cardboard to form a stencil.

Seal the stencil with carpenter's glue or varnish.

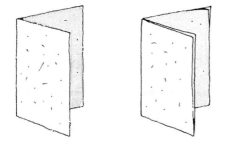

Fold 5½" x 8½" card in half or 8½" x 11" paper into quarters.

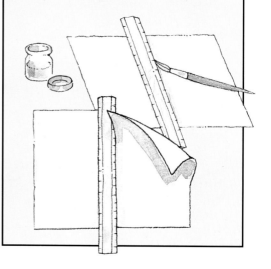

Fold paper into three and secure with ribbon.

Cards

There are three basic ways to make handmade paper cards that will fit in a standard-size envelope:

1. Folding dry paper to the required size.
2. Tearing dry paper to the required size.
3. Forming thicker paper card at the sheet-forming or couching stage.

Folding. A 5½" x 8½" sheet can be folded in half. The front can be plain or decorated with a simple design, and a message written inside.

An 8½" x 11" sheet can be folded in four. Once it is folded twice, even thin paper will be strong enough to stand upright. After folding, mark the front and inside sections lightly with a pencil and open the folded sheet out flat. (Bear in mind that the lettering and design will be facing in opposite directions — while working on the one, the other will be upside down and diagonally opposite.)

Paper can also be folded in three across its width. Divide the paper into three (for an 8½" x 11" sheet each panel will be about 3¾" inches wide), score along the fold-lines with a bone folder and fold the panels inwards so that they overlap.

Note: When measuring paper for folding, take into account the total width of the paper, including any furry deckle edges. If you fold too tightly, these edges will be squashed.

Tearing. An 8½" x 11" sheet of paper can also be torn in half to make two 5½" 8½" sheets. Alternatively it can be torn in four to make smaller 4¼" x 5½" cards, suitable for invitations. Bear in mind, however, that the paper needs to be thicker than that made in the

Note: Never cut visible edges of handmade paper, as it destroys the effect. Tearing handmade paper is a useful skill that is invaluable when tearing any quality paper (such as Fabriano or Arches'). First, firmly hold a ruler against the fold-line and score the paper with a bone folder or smooth, blunt knife. Then fold the paper along the scored crease and smooth the crease with a bone folder or back of a spoon. Fold the paper along the crease in the opposite direction and smooth it as before. The thicker the paper, the more folding will be necessary before tearing. To tear the paper, open it out and hold a ruler firmly against the fold with one hand. Grasp the opposite top corner of the page with the other hand and tear downwards slowly. The torn edge should resemble a deckle edge.

Another method of tearing can be used in the case of thin paper such as Japanese paper or lightweight handmade paper. Simply mark the line you wish to tear with a thin pencil and lightly brush along it with a wet paintbrush. When the water has soaked through to the back of the paper, tear along the line. You will now have a soft rather than a hard edge. The advantage of this method is that it also enables you to tear on a curve.

projects so far. A disadvantage of tearing larger sheets to make smaller cards is that you lose the unique character of the soft deckle edge.

Making thicker paper or card while couching.
By increasing the amount of pulp in a vat, you will automatically form thicker sheets. Alternatively, couch two or three sheets of wet paper one on top of another [*see* Chapter 9 for laminating techniques]. This is easier than it sounds, as each sheet of wet paper will naturally bond to the sheet below. The trick is to line up the mold accurately on top of the previously couched sheet and then to couch as usual.

Mountcards for photographs
Handmade paper cards form an attractive background for photographs. A novel idea for Christmas cards is to send family snapshots mounted on handmade cards. The handmade paper will tend to be stiff enough to stand as a card and can be formed at the couching stage either by using thick pulp, or by laminating two or three sheets. When dry, fold the 8½" x 11" or 5½" x 8½" sheet

Mark off the position of the photograph with a pencil and cut diagonal slits in the card for inserting the corners of the photograph.

in half, using a bone folder to score the fold, and position the photograph centrally on the front of the card. Mark the corners with a thin pencil line and remove the photograph. Then mark a point on each line ½ inch from the corner and

Thick paper cards make unique mounts for photographs.

at each corner draw a diagonal line joining the two points. Carefully cut along these lines with a knife and insert the photograph by tucking the corners into the slits.

Art cards

Creative and colorful cards making the most of your artistic or design abilities can be created at the couching stage. Two methods will be outlined.

1. Squirting away the pulp

REQUIREMENTS
Plant mister
A tub of thick pulp
A tub of thin pulp in a contrasting color

Using a mold and deckle, form a fairly thick basic sheet in one color and couch it onto wet felt. Wash away any pulp adhering to the mold and form a second sheet in a contrasting color, using thinner pulp. Once the sheet has drained sufficiently, raise the mold to a vertical posi-

Spraying away the pulp with a jet of water.

tion and spray a fine jet of water from the nozzle of the plant mister at it, either in random squiggles or controlled lines. This is best done outside, as the sprayed pulp will be plastered over your walls if you work inside. For added effect, spatter small 'watermarks' onto the mold, creating a textured surface on the paper. When you are happy with your pattern, couch it carefully on top of the first base sheet and cover

Art cards made by squirting away the pulp or by creating wet paper collages.

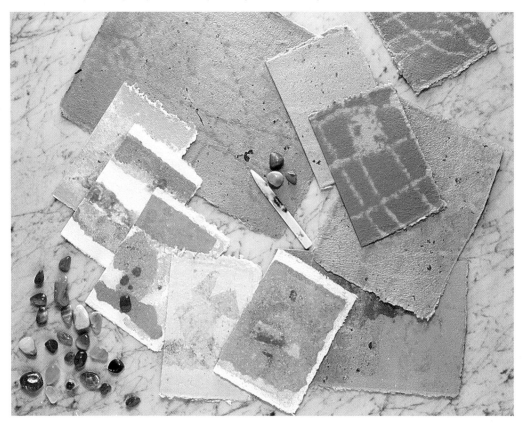

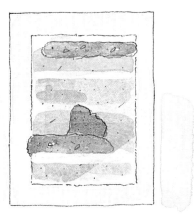

design and continue with the next one, until you have a post ready to press. Finally hang up the felts to dry.

Folded card holder

Handmade paper can be folded in unusual ways to highlight the attractive deckle edge. For example, insert a sheet of contrasting, hand-made or commercial paper, cut to size, in the folded paper for your message. The card holder can be further enhanced by tying it with a satin ribbon or twisted gold thread. Unless you intend writing on them, these card holders need not be sized.

Rectangular folded card holder

REQUIREMENTS
Sheet of handmade paper, 8½" x 11"
Contrasting paper, 3¾" x 5¾"

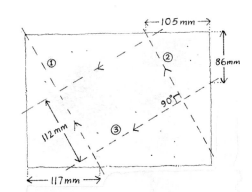

Diagram of fold-lines for rectangular card holder.

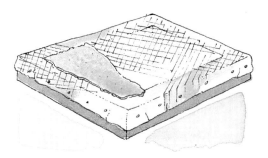

Position torn strips of paper onto the newly couched sheet. Dip a corner of the mold into thin pulp and couch it onto the collage.

it with another wet felt. Continue in this manner until you have made enough cards, press the pile of felts as usual and hang up to dry.

2. Wet paper collages

REQUIREMENTS
Previously made handmade paper
A tub of thick pulp
One or two tubs of thin pulp in contrasting colors

Using the thick pulp, form and couch a base sheet onto wet felt. On this wet sheet, place torn strips of handmade or tissue paper, and allow the moisture to seep through and dampen these strips. Then wash off the pulp adhering to the mold and dip an edge (or corner) of the mold into a tub of thin colored pulp. Couch this somewhere on the base sheet and torn paper in such a way that the overlapping fibers of the pulp trap the torn paper. Continue in this way, layering the thin colored pulp, until you are satisfied with the design. Lay a felt over the

86 mm = 3⅜"
105 mm = 4⅛"
112 mm = 4⅜"
117 mm = 6½"

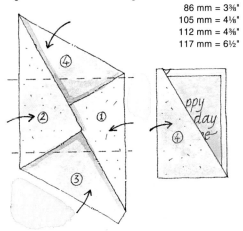

Fold the sides inwards in the order as numbered, tuck the flaps into one another and insert a message card.

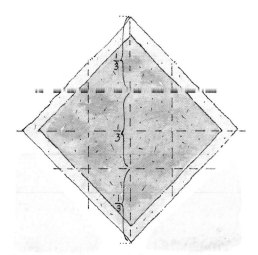

Position the smaller square in the center of the larger one and score fold-lines.

Square and round card holders

Copy the fold-lines in the diagram onto a plain piece of paper to act as a guide. Lay the 8½" x 11" sheet of handmade paper over the plain paper and turn in the sides as indicated.

Square card holder

REQUIREMENTS
One sheet of handmade paper, 8 inches square
One sheet of handmade paper in a contrasting
    color, 7 inches square
Commercial card
Satin ribbon or twisted thread, 20 inches long

Form square sheets by making either a square mold or square templates in the same way as the envelope template. When dry, position the smaller square centrally over the larger one, using double-sided tape or folded adhesive tape, and fold as indicated in the diagram. Note where the fold-lines divide the square in three. (The diagram can be enlarged on a photocopier to the size you require, and the fold-lines marked off on your paper with a bone folder.) Inside the folded square, insert a message on a piece of

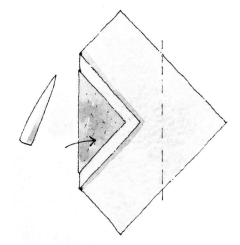

Fold sides towards the center

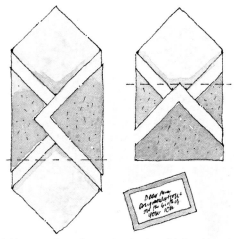

Fold corners inwards, overlapping by a third and insert a message card.

card. For added effect, mark a colored border round the edge of the card with a felt-tipped pen.

Round card holders

There are two basic ways to make these cards:

Method 1

REQUIREMENTS
The same as for the square card holder, but using two circular sheets in contrasting colors, one with a diameter about 1 inch less than the other.

Round paper can be made on an embroidery frame with net curtaining stretched over it, or by using a circular template. Stick down the smaller circle in the center of the larger one with double-sided tape and fold as indicated. Note that the edges are folded to the center of the circle on all four sides. Insert the message

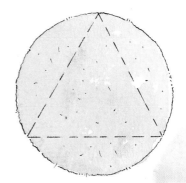

Draw an equilateral triangle inside the circle and fold the edges towards the center.

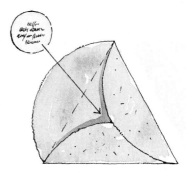

Insert a message card and tuck the last flap under the first.

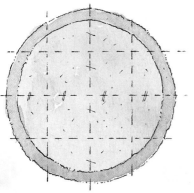

Position the smaller circle in the center of the larger one and score fold-lines.

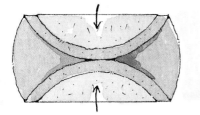

Fold the edges towards the center.

Insert a message and tie the card with a ribbon.

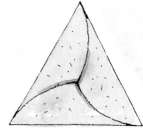

card into the card holder and tie a ribbon or twisted thread around it for a finishing touch.

Method 2

REQUIREMENTS
Compass
Round sheet of handmade paper
Commercial card

On a piece of paper, draw a circle the size of the handmade sheet. Set the compass at radius length and divide the circumference of the circle into three. Draw an equilateral triangle inside the circle (the sides of the triangle will also form the fold-lines). Using this as a guide, fold the sheet of handmade paper, smoothing the folds firmly with a bone folder. Insert a

Several sheets of paper can be joined in one long strip to make a zigzag Japanese fold-card.

triangular or circular message card and tuck the flaps of the paper into one another as shown.

Japanese folded card

REQUIREMENTS
Three to five sheets of 5½" x 8½" (or smaller) handmade paper

This is an attractive way to use 5½" x 8½" (or smaller) sheets of paper. Fold the sheets of paper in half and overlap them by half the sheet, butting up to the fold. Make sure that all the edges line up when the card is folded before gluing. Press the folded card under weights for 24 hours. The card can be inserted into an envelope as is, or can be threaded with a long

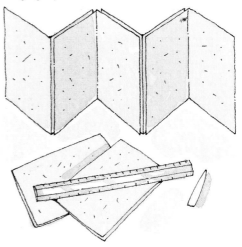

Overlap the folded sheets of paper by half each time, butting up to the fold.

ribbon. Punch holes in the card and pull the ribbon through, taking care not to tear the paper. Sized paper will be less likely to tear.

Containers for gifts

Handmade paper makes an attractive wrapping for gifts, giving them a unique, personal touch.

Simple bags

REQUIREMENTS
Rectangular paper

Following the instructions in the diagram, first fold the sides of the paper towards the center, with an overlap of ½ inch. Smooth the folds at the sides with a bone folder, glue down the overlap at the center and press under weights for an hour. Then draw foldlines 1 inch from both sides on the back and the front, and score with a bone folder. Fold towards the inside of the bag, pressing down well. Mark a fold-line 1½ inches from the bottom and tear away the inner part of the flap as illustrated. Glue down the flap and press under weights for 24 hours.

Pillow box

REQUIREMENTS
As for Simple bags

Draw the shape of the box on a spare piece of paper, marking fold-lines as dotted lines. Either use this as a guide for cutting and folding the handmade paper, or for making a template to use on a mold. Crease all fold-lines, fold the box in half on the center fold-line and glue the flap under the opposite side. Place under weights for an hour. Then fold the top flaps inward to close the box. The box can be further enhanced by tying a satin ribbon around it.

Pillow box and gift bags.

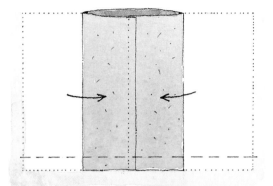

Fold both sides inwards to overlap at the center.

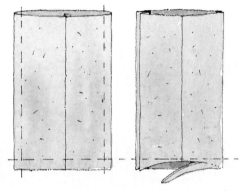

Tear away lower edge in a curve to reduce bulk.

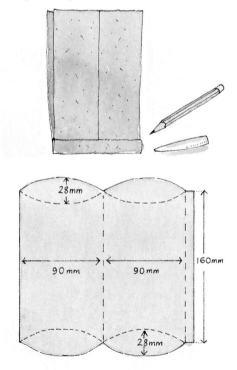

Diagram for pillow box. (28 mm = 1"; 90 mm = 3½"; 160 mm = 6½")

Gift box

REQUIREMENTS
Thick cardboard
Two sheets of 8¼" x 11" handmade paper

You can cover existing boxes, or make your own according to the diagram. To make your own, mark out the base measurements of the box on a piece of cardboard, making sure that all lines are perpendicular to each other. Measure the sides of the box and add this measurement to that of the four sides of the base. Cut out the shape, fold along all scored lines and tape the corners together. To cover the box, mark out the basic box template on a sheet of handmade paper, allowing an extra ½ inch to the height of the sides for folding down inside the box. Add tuck-in flaps for gluing around the corners of the box. Apply glue to the handmade paper, working radially from the center. Position the box centrally on the paper and press well. Glue the paper to the two shorter sides, folding over the top of the box and smoothing the flaps around the corners. Then glue the remaining two sides. Press well with your fingers and turn the margin over the top edge. Follow the same procedure for a lid, but note that the lid will be slightly larger (about ¹⁄₁₆ inch all around) than the box, in order to fit over it. Measure carefully before cutting either the cardboard or the handmade paper.

Alternatively, cover an existing box with handmade paper. Simply open the box out flat and mark off the measurements of the base and sides on handmade paper, allowing an extra margin for tucking in at the top. On the two opposite shorter sides, draw 'tuck-in' flaps for folding under the longer sides at the corners. Cut out the covering paper and spread paste over it with a brush. Position the box carefully in the center and glue down the shorter sides. Finally, turn in the top margins. For a special gift box, you may first want to cover the inside of the box with marbled paper (see Chapter 9).

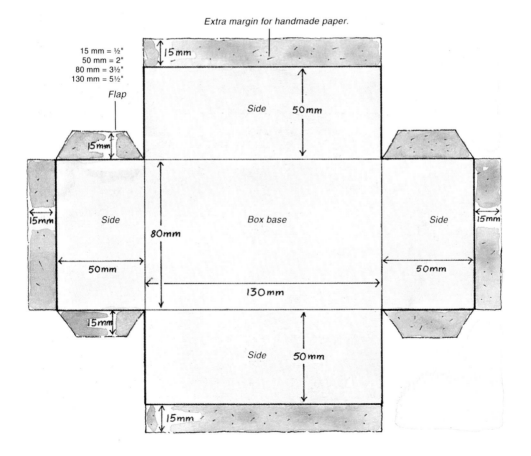

Extra margin for handmade paper.

15 mm = ½"
50 mm = 2"
80 mm = 3½"
130 mm = 5½"

15 mm

Flap

15 mm

Side   50 mm

15 mm   Side   Box base   Side   15 mm

80 mm

50 mm   50 mm

130 mm

15 mm

Side   50 mm

15 mm

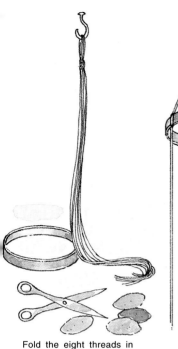

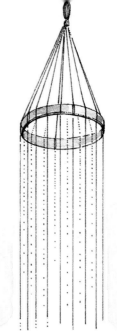

Fold the eight threads in half and tie a knot 2½" from the center.

Tie every fourth thread to the embroidery frame.

Tie the remaining threads to the frame, spacing them evenly.

Tie the paper ovals in a spiral.

Paper mobile

A colorful paper mobile can be an attractive addition to a child's room or a fun housewarming gift for a friend. Little scrolls of plant papers wrapped in silver thread, small animal shapes, colorful circles or squares can be hung from wire or an embroidery frame. The lightness of paper, and its exciting color and texture combinations, can be an artistic accent as it moves gently in a breeze at an open window or doorway.

REQUIREMENTS
Embroidery frame, 8 inches in diameter
Crochet cotton
Darning needle
Paint
Clear matt varnish
Paintbrush
Turpentine
Thick pulps in a variety of colors
Wallpaper paste, mixed according to the instructions on the package

Without using a frame, pour thick pulp onto dry felt in a roughly oval shape 3–4 inches long. Use as many colors as you have to make 16 such paper ovals. Lay another dry felt on top and mop carefully with a sponge until you have removed the excess water. Replace the now damp top felt with a dry one and roll gently with a rolling pin. Remove the top felt and leave the paper ovals to dry on the base felt. When dry, place the ovals on newspaper and paint one side of each oval with wallpaper paste. When they are dry, paint the other side.

Meanwhile, paint the embroidery frame in a color matching the ovals, applying two coats of paint, and then two coats of clear varnish. Remember to clean the brush with turpentine after use.

To assemble the mobile, first cut eight 6–foot lengths of crochet cotton. Fold the bundle of threads in half and tie a knot in the center, so that you have a 2½ inch loop to hang on a hook. Hang the bundle of threads at a convenient height, ready for tying on the embroidery frame. Tie the 1st, 5th, 9th and 13th strands of cotton onto the frame about 1 foot away from the central knot, dividing the frame into four equal portions. Make sure that the frame hangs level: adjust the knots if necessary. Then tie on the other strands of thread, spacing them evenly round the frame. Decide on the color order of your ovals, pierce a hole in the first one and tie it up so that it hangs about 5 inches from the frame. Repeat this procedure with the next oval, but tie it so that it hangs slightly lower than the first oval. Continue in this manner until you have created a spiral effect with your ovals. To complete the mobile, cut off all loose ends of cotton.

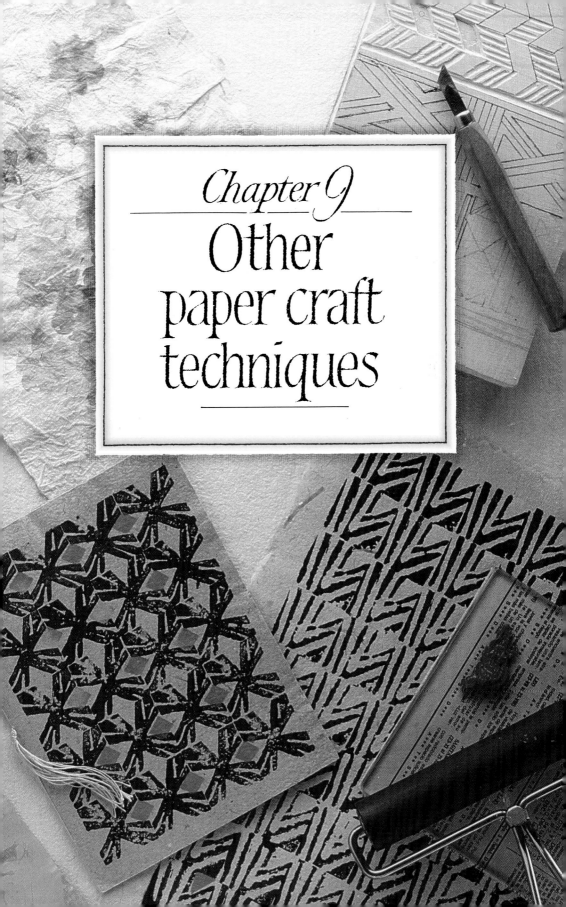

Chapter 9

Other paper craft techniques

Some of the crafts in this chapter require more specialized equipment and techniques. However, many exciting and original things can be done with handmade paper, leading you on to fascinating experiments with paper as an art form.

Handmade paper can be used as a mount for old photographs, either as a card as shown in Chapter 8, or within a frame. Laminating several sheets on top of one another creates thicker paper or card. This can be taken a step further, creating interesting surface textures by laminating objects between the sheets. Other raised surface designs can be created by means of embossing or embedding objects in the paper. Unsized paper is an excellent surface for printing on and printed handmade paper can, for example, make attractive cards, book covers, patterns for bags and boxes. Once you have accumulated a collection of beautiful handmade sheets, you can also bind them in a book.

Mounts for old photographs
Plant paper or onion-skin paper is particularly effective as a background for old family photographs.

REQUIREMENTS
Ready-made wooden frame
Wood stain (medium oak)
Wood sealer
Paintbrush, ½ inch wide
Gold poster paint
Very small paintbrush (No. 0)
Mounting-board

Sand the frame if necessary, stain it with wood stain and leave it to dry. You may want to apply more than one coat, depending on the shade you require. Cut the mounting-board to fit inside the frame, using a knife and steel ruler. Either position the sheet of handmade paper so that the deckle edge is visible (with a good margin all round), or cut it to fit the frame. Then cut the photograph to the size you require, position it centrally on the paper and mark the top corners with a thin pencil line as a guide for gluing down. For an attractive 'antique' finish, rule an edge of gold paint around the photograph with a paintbrush or gold felt-tipped pen.

Apply double-sided tape to the back of the photograph and position it carefully on the handmade paper, using the pencil marks as a guide. Press it under weights for 24 hours, then assemble the frame, glass, mounting-board and handmade paper and fasten securely with pins or nails. Finally seal the back of the frame with strips of masking tape overlapping the mounting-board. For a professional finish, you could cover the back of the frame with brown paper.

Laminating and embossing
These two techniques involve working with newly formed wet sheets at the time of couching. Embossing works equally well with both the pouring and couching method of papermaking.

Laminating refers either to couching two or more sheets one on top of the other for extra thickness and to prevent cockling, or to sandwiching objects between the two sheets. For the best results, keep the pulp fairly thin. After couching one sheet onto a wet felt, position a flat object or objects on the wet sheet and couch a second sheet on top, sandwiching the object or objects between the two sheets. Anything from bits of wool, lace, string, feathers, ferns, pressed leaves and flowers, pine needles, torn tissue paper or cut-out letters could be placed between the sheets. For added interest paint the object(s) first — the paint will bleed through the paper, creating an interesting effect. Bear in mind that the color of autumn leaves will run when sandwiched between two wet sheets of paper. It can look very beautiful, but if you want to eliminate this, boil and press the leaves first.

Embossing refers to a raised surface or relief design in paper, as is often used for company or personal logos, wedding invitations, etc. A sheet of damp paper, pressed onto a relief design, retains the image. You can use natural objects such as those listed under laminating for relief designs, or manufactured designs such as linoleum block prints, cut-out letters, woven raffia or cane work.

First couch a sheet of paper onto thin fabric such as nonwoven dressmaker's interfacing or a man's handkerchief, and hang it up to dry for four to six hours to speed up the drying process. Then, while the paper is still slightly damp, lay an object such as a leaf, feather or fern on top of it. Cover it with another piece of dry fabric and iron the paper dry. The object will cause an impression on the paper.

Alternatively, you could allow the damp paper to dry naturally on top of its relief object. Position the damp sheet of paper (still backed with its fabric) *over* the object on stiff board or cardboard, and gently peel the fabric away. Lay a piece of foam (about ¾ inch thick) over the damp paper and cover it with a board and weights for 24 hours. Remove the weights and board and carefully lift the foam to check. If the paper is still damp, cover it with a dry piece of foam (or possibly newspaper) and press it again. Do not lift or remove the paper until it is bone-dry and the image pressed into it well.

Another embossing technique is to couch a sheet of paper directly onto a relief object such as a linoleum block print. First prepare the block by spraying it with non-stick baking spray or rubbing the surface with talcum powder. Allow the wet sheets to dry completely before removing them.

String embossing with papyrus paper.

Simple printing on unsized paper

Printing techniques that work particularly well on unsized handmade paper are potato-cuts, linoleum blocks and woodcuts.

Potato-cut printing

REQUIREMENTS
Potato
Container with a flat base (for example a plastic margarine tub)
Piece of thin sponge or foam rubber to fit in the tub
Powdered paint
Unsized paper

Lay out newspapers on a table as protection against the mess. Slice the potato in half cleanly, making sure that you have a smooth printing surface. Cut one half into a square shape. (At this point you can cut a handle to the potato to grip with.) Cut a few strips out of the potato in the design of your choice. Do not spend too much time worrying about a design — even the simplest or crudest of shapes can develop into the most exciting patterns when printed. Using a soft pencil, mark a light horizontal and vertical line on the unsized paper, slightly off-center in each case. This acts

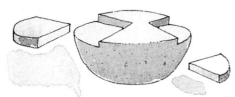

Cut wedges out of the potato to create a design.

Cut a 'handle' on the potato.

Ink up the potato by pressing it onto the printing pad.

as a guide for the first row of printing. Mix a little powdered paint with water in the plastic tub (try three heaping teaspoons of powder in a little water as a start), and press the sponge into it to soak up the paint. Turn over the sponge — this is your printing pad. Now press the cut surface of the potato block firmly onto the sponge and then onto the newspaper to see how it prints. Make adjustments to the block and to the density of the paint and do another test print. When you are satisfied with the thickness of the paint and the shape of the block, print your first row of potato prints, lining them up against one of the pencil lines. Either ink up the block with each printing or print two at a time. The second print will be slightly lighter in shade and can give an interesting texture to the pattern.

Linoleum block cutting

REQUIREMENTS
Linoleum-block or wood-cutting tools (available at hobby shops)
Linoleum
Oil-based ink
Roller
A piece of glass or a ceramic tile
Spoon

Draw a design on paper and transfer it to the linoleum by rubbing the back of the paper with a soft pencil or by slipping a piece of carbon between it and the linoleum, and retracing the lines with a pen. Mark in the areas you want to print and cut away the remainder. Before cutting, put the linoleum in the sun or in a warm spot to soften it — it will then be easier to cut. Be careful to cut away from you, otherwise you could cut yourself badly if the knife slips. For printing, first squeeze a teaspoonful of ink onto the surface of the glass (or tile) and spread it well with the roller. Then, using the roller, spread the ink over the block until the raised surface is evenly inked up. Carefully lay the sheet of unsized, handmade paper over the block and press it down gently with the flat of your hand. Then rub the entire area with the back of a spoon to ensure that the whole surface of the block makes good contact with the paper. To check whether the impression has taken, carefully lift a corner of the paper. When you are satisfied with the result, gently peel off the paper and lay it flat to dry.

Simple marbling

Marbling is the technique whereby a colored pattern that resembles marble is transferred onto paper. It is associated mainly with bookbinding and the lining of gift boxes, but can also be used to create colorful notepaper and envelopes, folders or cards. Marbling relies on the fact that oil and water do not mix. Oil paints are floated on water and manipulated into a pattern. A sheet of paper is then laid on the surface and picks up the pattern. Usually commercial papers are used for this technique but handmade paper can be successfully marbled provided that it is well sized and has been allowed to 'stand' for a while. Such paper is particularly attractive as a background for hand-embroidery. The simplest method, using a minimum of equipment or expensive ingredients, is outlined below.

REQUIREMENTS

*Shallow tray such as a cat litter tray or roasting
    pan*
Oil paints in two colors
Turpentine
Two small jars for mixing colors
Two paintbrushes
Skewer or thin stick
Newspapers
Commercial or sized handmade paper

Fill the tray with cold water to a depth of about 3 inches. Keep some newspapers — laid out flat — close by. Squeeze about 1 inch of oil paint from each tube into a jar, one color per jar. Add about 1 tablespoon of turpentine to each color and mix until the paint has the consistency of thin cream. Dip a paintbrush into the first color and drop some paint onto the surface of the water to test its consistency. It should spread to about 1 inch in diameter. If the patch shrinks, the paint is too thick and needs to be thinned with more turpentine. If the patch spreads too wide and too fast, the paint is too thin and some more needs to be added.

When the consistency is right, drop paint randomly over the whole surface of the water by tapping the handle of the paintbrush against the side of the tray. Repeat with the second color. To create a pattern, simply drag a skewer through the water in a slow zig-zag motion. Do not stir too much, or the paint will break up and become spotty. Lift your paper by grasping two diagonally opposite corners and lower it gently onto the surface of the water, smoothing out the sheet from the center to the corners. Make certain that there are no trapped air bubbles, as these will create blanks spots in your pattern. While smoothing out the bubbles, be sure not to submerge the paper.

Now lift out the paper carefully and lay it on the newspaper to dry, with the pattern side up. Between each printing, remove the excess paint from the surface of the water with rolled-up newspaper and repeat the process. When the marbled paper is dry, it can be pressed in a heavy book or under weights for a few days.

> *Note:* An alternative method of marbling is to 'tie-dye' handmade paper. This is done by scrunching up the paper, tying it into a ball and immersing it in colored dye for 2–4 hours. Allow the paper to dry thoroughly before carefully unwrapping the ball. When it is open, the process can be repeated with another color, or the paper can be smoothed out and pressed under weights for a few days.

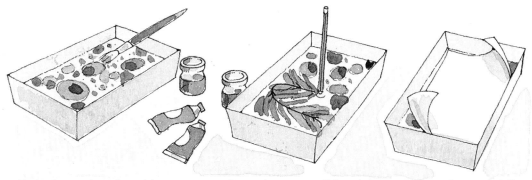

Drop paint onto the surface of the water.

Drag a skewer or pencil through the water to create a pattern.

Lower the paper onto the surface of the water.

Simple bookbinding

When you have accumulated a large quantity of handmade papers of varied texture and color, you may wish to bind them in a beautiful leather binding. However, it is not necessary to bind it professionally to create an object of beauty. There are simple but very effective ways to bind books, even if you have no experience and only the minimum of equipment.

If you are a calligrapher, you could write quotes or poems in the books and turn them into treasured heirlooms.

REQUIREMENTS
Plain or patterned handmade or commercial paper for the cover
Buttonhole silk or crochet cotton (No. 10)
Thin darning needle
Six sheets of handmade paper
A pair of dividers

Fold the sheets of handmade paper in half and crease the fold firmly. Slip the pages inside one another to form a section. Mark out the measurements of the cover, allowing ⅛ inch outside the deckle edges at the head and tail, and ⅜ inch at the fore-edge. You will trim it later. Cut out the cover with a knife and steel ruler, then fold it in half and crease the fold with a bone folder. Slip the section inside the cover, leaving an equal margin at the top and bottom. Open out the book to the center fold, find the center point on the fold and mark it with a pencil. Measure 1 inch up from the tail and down from the head, and mark these points with a pencil. Check that the book still fits well into the cover and that the margins are still equal all round.

Using the darning needle, prick three holes through all layers of paper, including the cover. Cut a piece of thread 10 inches long, thread it through the needle and begin sewing through the middle hole in the center of the book. Follow the diagram, sewing in a S-formation, until you push the needle through the center hole again. Tie a knot in the thread and cut off the ends to about ½ inch. Close the book and mark a point on the inside cover at the fore-edge, allowing a ⅛ inch margin from the deckle edge. Use a pair of dividers (or strip of paper) to mark this measurement from the edge of the cover to act as a guide for cutting. Finally, cut the cover at the fore-edge with a knife and steel ruler. Press under weights for a week.

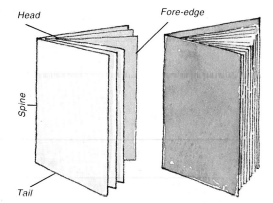

Slip the folded pages inside one another to form a section and slip the section insider the cover.

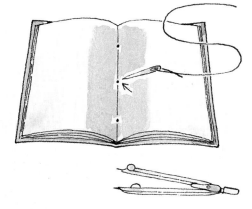

Prick three holes through the layers of paper and cover, and begin sewing through the middle hole.

Sew through the holes following the diagram.

Opposite: Simple bookbinding: single-section and Japanese fold-books. The cover at top of page is a paper-cast of a woodcut, done by Thelma Harwood.

From left to right: Japanese fold-book in Kozo fiber, concertina fold-book made from overlapping 8½" x 11" sheet and miniature fold-book.

Japanese fold-book

A Japanese 'concertina' fold-book makes a lovely gift and is particularly charming when done as a miniature. It can be left blank for the recipient to write in, or could contain a poem or a short illustrated story for a child. The book can be made with one long strip of paper or by joining several sheets together. Below are the instructions for making a miniature out of one sheet of 8½" x 11" handmade paper torn into three strips.

REQUIREMENTS
A sheet of handmade 8½" x 11" paper
Wallpaper paste
Stiff cardboard for cover
Marbled commercial or handmade paper for
*   cover*
Waxed paper or wastepaper
Small paintbrush (about No. 2)

Mix the wallpaper paste by stirring 1 teaspoon of powder into 1 cup of water. Let it stand for 24 hours. Stir occasionally. Then divide your 8½" x 11" sheet lengthwise in three columns, each 2¾ inches wide, and mark the paper with a light pencil line at top and bottom. Lay a ruler against the pencil marks as a guide for the tear line, brush lightly with a wet paintbrush against the ruler and tear along the line. Repeat for the second tear. Now fold each strip carefully in

four, smoothing the creases with the bone folder as you go. To join the three strips, simply overlap a page at both ends of one strip with a page from each of the other stirps and glue down firmly. Fold the paper so that it 'concertinas', with folds facing alternatively front and back. When glued and folded, press under weights for 24 hours.

The cover is made from two identical pieces of cardboard, covered with decorative paper. To make the cover, draw up each cover on the cardboard with a pencil, allowing a margin of about ⅛ inch all round the fold-book. Include all deckle edges in your measurements. Check that the sides are squared and parallel and cut the cardboard with a knife. Make sure that both covers are identical and correct if necessary.

Now measure decorative paper for the cover, allowing an extra ½ inch wider than the cardboard all round. Spread paste over the covering paper by brushing it radially from the center. Remove the excess paper from the corners by cutting the paper diagonally approximately ⅛ inch away from the corner. Turn in the top and bottom flaps (head and tail) and press firmly against the cardboard. Neatly tuck in the corner folds where they overlap the side flaps with a bone folder (see diagram). Then fold in the two side flaps, pressing well. Place a sheet of waxed paper on either side of the cover, and press under weights for 24 hours.

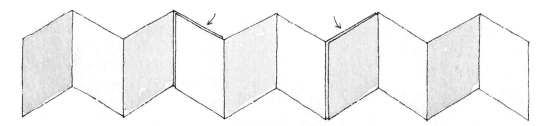

Join the strips by overlapping a page at each end.

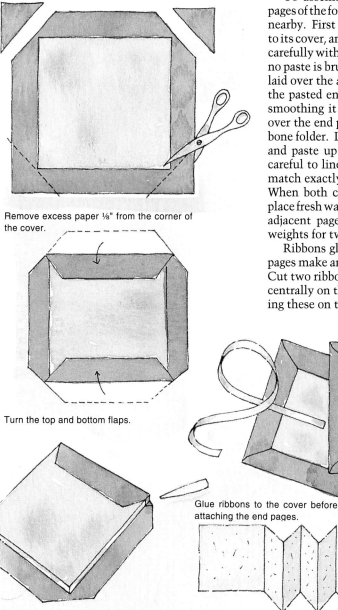

Remove excess paper ⅛" from the corner of the cover.

Turn the top and bottom flaps.

Tuck in the corner folds neatly against the card with a bone folder.

Glue ribbons to the cover before attaching the end pages.

Glue end pages to each cover.

To assemble the book, open out the end pages of the folded book, keeping the two covers nearby. First paste up one end page and glue it to its cover, and then the other. Apply the paste carefully with a paintbrush, and make sure that no paste is brushed over the fold. Waxed paper laid over the adjoining page may help. Attach the pasted end page centrally onto the cover, smoothing it down well. Place waxed paper over the end page and rub down firmly with a bone folder. Leave the waxed paper where it is and paste up the other cover. Be especially careful to line up the two covers so that they match exactly before gluing the second cover. When both covers are attached to the book, place fresh waxed paper between the covers and adjacent pages of the book and press under weights for two to three days.

Ribbons glued between the covers and end pages make an attractive addition to the cover. Cut two ribbons 16 inches long and glue them centrally on the two inside covers before pasting these on the end pages.

Chapter 10
Paper art

Many people imagine that 'paper art' techniques involve origami, paper cut-outs, paper collages, puppets, stage sets or papier-mâché. However, while paper art is none of these things specifically, it can include several elements of each of them.

As in the case of origami, paper cut-outs or collages, dry paper can be folded, cut, torn, punctured, sewn, woven, embossed and painted to form assemblages and collages with unusual tactile depth and richness. Damp paper can be laid over sculpted forms in a way that resembles puppet-making. Large assemblages and constructions may have the flavor of stage set design. However, papier-mâché bears the closest resemblance to much of what is understood as paper art, for it involves working with the basic paper pulp itself.

Wet paper pulp has a unique flexibility and three-dimensional quality different from any other art medium. Wet pulp resembles sloppy bread dough, filling in spaces and faithfully reproducing the shape and texture of the surface against which it dries. One can embed objects in it, or it can be cast into molds or poured thickly in abstract designs with exciting colors and textures. Thick, drained pulp can be easily manipulated by pressing shapes into it, or heaping it so as to create raised surfaces. It can also be modeled and shaped in a fairly controlled fashion, similar to clay. This quality lends itself to an art form known as paper sculpture.

In addition, by using the couching method, thin translucent sheets of tinted paper can be layered to create depth and subtle color combinations, sometimes revealing laminated objects underneath the surface. Partially dried paper can be overlapped, folded or twisted, creating interesting relief patterns of light and shade. In combination with other media, such as embroidery, weaving, lettering, pastels, pottery and sculpture, paper is beginning to capture the attention of artists in both the East and West.

Paper art techniques can be time-consuming, often requiring long drying periods or elaborate equipment or constructions. This chapter aims to give you an idea of some of the possibilities of the medium, using simple equipment. None of these projects takes up too much time. Once you have tried some of these techniques your imagination is sure to stimulate further experimentation of your own.

The 'R' is taken from a plaster cast of lettering done in sand. The alphabet is cast from a woodcut by Martin Field.

Paper-casting

Thick paper pulp can be poured over a variety of textured and relief surfaces to create intriguing paper-casts.

REQUIREMENTS
A bucket of pulp (plain white or tinted)
Frame or strips of wood
Two pieces of felt or fabric
Jug
Rolling pin
Absorbent sponge
Interesting surfaces or objects
Net bag or sieve
Non-stick baking spray

Drain the pulp through a net bag or sieve until it is quite thick, but still runny enough to be poured. Choose an interesting surface onto which to pour the pulp, such as a door mat, tree trunk, pile of stones or shells, patterned beach sand, tire tread, flotsam and jetsam picked up on the beach, wood carving, printing block or sculpture, or create your own surface. To make your own molded surface, place objects such as twisted rope, folded fabric, pottery chips, seed pods or stones on a wooded board. Spray all surfaces that will be in contact with the pulp with non-stick baking spray. Position a wooden frame around the objects and pour a thick layer of pulp into it. Spread the layer evenly with your fingers and make sure that all raised areas are covered.

Place a piece of felt or fabric over the pulp and press down gently. Mop up the excess water seeping through the fabric with a sponge until the pulp is compressed and firm. At this point reinforce any thin, weak areas with more pulp. Gently remove the frame and replace the wet felt with a dry one. Press the dry felt down gently to absorb more water, then press more firmly with a rolling pin. Remove the felt and place the paper cast in the sun to dry. Depending on the weather and size of the mold, this should take between one and three days.

Make your own casting mold

There are several ways of making your own casting mold, using plasticine, plaster of Paris, rubber latex, or cardboard cut-outs.

❑ Plasticine is excellent for creating a simple casting mold. When making intricate designs, however, the plasticine tends to come away with the pulp when you remove the cast. Warm the plasticine in the sun or other warm spot for 15-30 minutes to soften it, and then roll it out flat on a board with a rolling pin. Press objects such as nails, forks, corks, cookie cutters, wrought iron, bent wire or beads into the plasticine. This can be quite random, as the effects created when pouring plain or colored pulp into a three-dimensional mold can be surprisingly effective, even if the indentations in the plasticine are made quite casually.

You may leave the randomly shaped plasticine as it is, or cut it into a square or rectangular shape with a sharp knife. You can then pour directly onto the mold (creating an irregular edge), or make a frame around your 'casting mold' to contain the pulp. Simply cut a 1¼-inch strip of cardboard long enough to make a frame around the plasticine, and glue or tape the two ends together. Pour pulp into the mold as above and place it in the sun to dry.

❑ Plaster of Paris will form a more solid and permanent mold, suitable for several castings. Mix the plaster of Paris in the ratio of 1 part plaster of Paris to 1 part water, adding the dry powder slowly to the water. The plaster can be poured over interesting objects or patterned beach sand to create a mold. You can create face masks by applying dampened surgical gauze to a greased face and spreading a layer of plaster of Paris over it. When it is dry, remove the mask, spread a second layer of plaster of Paris over it and leave to harden. Press paper pulp into this cast and leave to dry. For large molds, the plaster can be reinforced with fabric such as hessian or burlap.

❑ Cardboard cut-outs pasted on thick cardboard or wood are an inexpensive way to create a simple relief surface for casting paper pulp or 'laminate casting'. Corrugated cardboard also gives an interesting ribbed effect to the surface.

Plaster of Paris is poured onto sand and objects inside the frame.

Embedding objects in thick pulp

The opposite technique to the above is to pour thick pulp into an area defined by a frame and then press objects onto it. Then pour a little more pulp over to secure them. When the paper is dry, the fibers will cling to the objects, holding them in place. Moreover, some of the objects can be removed, leaving their shape embedded in the dry paper. Some objects can first be painted, or metal objects used. The latter will rust when in contact with the wet pulp and the rust stains will bleed interestingly into the wet pulp.

Pouring thick colored pulp onto a screen or board

Thick colored pulp can be poured onto a screen or board to form exciting variations in color and texture. When using a screen, the interest lies in the contrast between the texture of the upper surface and that created by the mesh, whereas in the case of the board, one sees the smooth flat surface created by the board.

1. Pouring thick pulp onto a silk screen or mold

REQUIREMENTS
A bucket of pulp, drained until very thick
Coloring agents
Milk cartons
Spoons for mixing colors
Mold or silk screen

Mix your colors in milk cartons using a little water, add 2 cups of drained pulp to each carton and stir well. Bear in mind that the wet color will be at least twice as intense as when the paper is dry. Leave the newly mixed colors to stand for at least two hours, as this helps prevent them from bleeding into each other on the screen.

Plan a design of colored bands or curves and begin pouring thick pulp over the screen. You can dispense with a frame to contain the pulp if you prefer a random edge. Make sure that the edges of the different colors mesh well, or you will have holes in your paper. To create straight edges, use strips of wood as containments for the pulp.

When your design is finished, remove excess water from the screen by carefully mopping the underside of the mesh with a sponge, and then lay the screen flat in the sun to dry. After a few hours it will be safe to tilt the screen onto its side. Depending on the weather, it should take 1–3 days to dry. Once dry, the piece can be further worked on by dripping thick pulp onto it or embedding fabric, wool, shells, seed pods and other oddments in it. When the piece is finished to your satisfaction, remove it from the screen by working round the edge with a knife.

A variation on the above method is to first pour thin white pulp over the entire screen as a foundation layer. When this layer is dry, you can pour the different colors of your design. This will strengthen the sheet and eliminate the problem of holes or thin areas appearing once the paper is dry.

> **Note:** *Another method of strengthening your sheet is to add premixed wallpaper paste to the pulp before pouring it onto the foundation layer on the screen. Wallpaper paste has the added advantage of preventing bacterial action in your pulp and discouraging attacks by insects. Add one cupful of premixed wallpaper paste to a bucket of drained pulp.*

2. Pouring thick pulp onto a board

REQUIREMENTS
As above, but use a board instead of a mold or screen
Piece of thin fabric or large felt

The advantage of this method is that you can draw a design on the board as a guide to applying the pulp. Furthermore the flat surface created by pouring onto smooth board can later be sized and used to write on. Follow the instructions for the screen method, but mop up excess water with a sponge *outside* the area of wet pulp as it is applied. When the entire design is complete, lay a piece of fabric over it and use a sponge to mop up the moisture seeping through the fabric. Once most of the excess water has been removed, lay the board flat in the sun to dry until it can safely be tilted onto its side without the pulp sliding off. When dry, slide a long knife between the paper and board and work it slowly and carefully under the paper until it lifts off cleanly.

> **Warning:** *For this method, do not add wallpaper paste to the pulp, or it will not come off the board.*

The translucent layers of the 'patchworking' method.

Paper collages

'Patchworking'

With this technique you use a mold to form sheets of paper and couch several overlapping sheets to make a bigger one: the edges overlap, bonding the paper together. This can form a base for some of the other techniques and can be particularly attractive if several different colors are used.

REQUIREMENTS

*Large piece of finely woven fabric, such as a
    bedsheet or tablecloth
Coloring agents
5½" x 8½" or 8½" x 11" mold
Bucket of plain pulp
Absorbent sponge
Four large plastic tubs*

First mix three colors of thick pulp in milk cartons and leave them to stand for two hours. Then prepare a tub of water containing 2 quarts of plain pulp, ready for forming sheets of paper. Wet the fabric thoroughly and stretch it out flat and straight onto a smooth surface, for example a kitchen table. Make sure that there are no air bubbles underneath. Form a sheet of paper with plain pulp, position the mold upside down somewhere on the fabric and use a sponge to mop up the excess water at the back of the screen (the side that is now uppermost). When it is no longer wet, lift one side of the mold gently to test whether it will come away, leaving the sheet on the fabric. If not, mop once more.

Make another sheet of paper and couch it next to the first in the same manner, overlapping an edge slightly. Mop as before. Continue in this way, overlapping the sheets to create a large sheet of paper in any shape or size you wish. Your only limit is the size of your fabric.

To apply overlapping colored layers, you will first need to dilute the colored pulp and stir it well to disperse the fibers. Pour a small quantity of the diluted colored pulp into the spare tubs and make thin colored sheets. For unusually shaped layers, either form whole sheets or merely dip an edge or corner of the mold into the pulp. Build up layers of overlapping thin, translucent sheets in different colors until you have created an interesting sheet of paper. This can form a colorful background for calligraphy or embroidery, or be made into a screen.

Making a screen

The overlap method for making large sheets of paper can be expanded to create interesting screens. Simply leave the paper on the fabric and size well, using one of the methods mentioned in Chapter 5. When the screen is dry, turn in a neat hem and nail or tack the fabric onto a wooden framework. If the paper has dried unevenly, size the paper and fabric again and gently stretch it to fit the frame. At this point, additional colors could be squirted or painted onto the paper to improve the design, or additional pieces of paper or fabric can be hand-embroidered onto it.

> *Note: The overlap technique can also be applied directly to a board. The advantage is that it will dry flat. It can then form a base for sculptural effects like twisted damp sheets (see p. 86).*

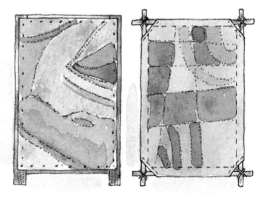
Tack fabric with its sheet of paper onto a wooden frame or sew a wide margin and thread bamboo sticks through all four sides.

Sculptural collages

Sculptural effects, by means of folding, twisting or scrunching damp sheets and applying them to a preformed wet sheet, can give a new dimension to the paper. Sculptural forms with contrasting textures can be added to paper either couched directly onto a board, or to wet paper left on the mold.

REQUIREMENTS

1½ quarts of prepared pulp
Thin dishcloths or pieces of nonwoven dressmaker's interfacing cut larger than your mold
Deckle-box and mold
Absorbent sponge

Using the deckle-box, make one or two sheets of paper, couch onto dishcloths or interfacing and hang up to dry in the sun for about an hour, or indoors for 3-5 hours. In the meantime, form another sheet of paper using the deckle-box. Leave it on the screen or couch it onto a board. Then, when the paper on the interfacing is still damp, but dry enough to be removed, slip a knife under one corner and peel the fabric away slightly. If the paper handles easily and is not too soggy and floppy, it is ready. If not, leave it

to dry for a little longer. Keep the preformed sheet on the mold or board nearby.

Remove the damp sheets from the fabric, one at a time, and fold or twist them into interesting shapes. Position them on the paper on the mold, applying a little pressure to make them stick. The preformed sheet on the mold should not be too dry for the sculpted sheets to stick successfully. For added interest, bits and pieces of previously made paper or interesting fabric can be soaked briefly and wedged in amongst the folds. Leave the mold to dry naturally, lying flat and away from strong heat. When the whole assemblage is dry, remove it carefully with a knife.

Constructions

By draping paper over sticks, bamboo or cane, you can create elaborate three-dimensional 'sculptures' that invite the eye to look beyond and behind the surface. This is particularly beautiful when working with thin translucent plant papers. The addition of beads, bones, shells, oddments of rolled paper, wool and fabric hung from the framework can turn the construction into a fascinating wall-hanging or mural.

Damp paper can be twisted and folded and attached to a wet sheet still on the mold.

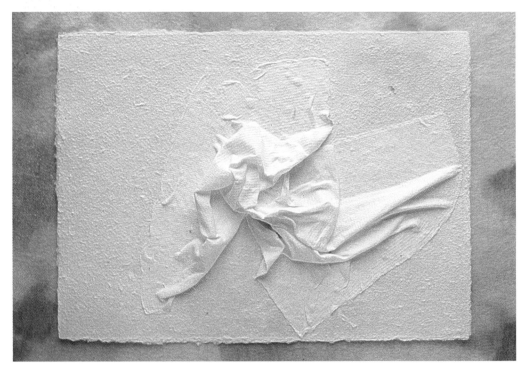

> **Note:** *An alternative way of draping paper over sticks is to tear and drape the paper while it is still damp. In this way it will shrink round the sticks as it dries. This is very effective when thin translucent plant papers are draped over a curved surface. When dry, it looks very good with a light shining behind it. Simply couch the paper directly onto a board, lift the entire sheet or part of it, and drape it over the construction. It helps to paint the sticks with wallpaper paste prior to draping to ensure a good strong bond.*

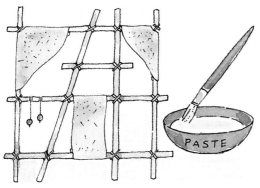

Draping paper over a stick or bamboo construction.

REQUIREMENTS
Dry preformed handmade paper
Sticks, bamboo or reed stems
Beige crochet cotton
Scissors
Premixed wallpaper paste
Paintbrush

Tie together the construction — either on one flat plane, or several layers of separate constructions. Lay a sheet of paper against a corner you wish to drape and mark off a tear line with a wet paintbrush. Allow a sufficient margin for folding round the sticks. Tear the paper and apply wallpaper paste to the edge of the paper and to the sticks that it will be in contact with. Drape the paper over the sticks immediately and fold it over. To ensure good contact, smooth over the contact points with the paintbrush. Continue in this manner, carefully planning where you want paper and where you want gaps. This is particularly important if you are working with several layers of constructions. When you are satisfied with the effect, you may want to add beads, shells, rolls of paper or other oddments for interest.

Bowls

Paper bowls are very satisfying to make, whether left plain, or painted with a design. Many artists incorporate sticks, beads, embroidery, masks and other sculptural effects in their bowls, turning them into works of art in their own right. There are two ways of casting bowls. The first is to apply thick paper pulp to the inner or outer surface of an existing bowl. The pulp may contain premixed wallpaper paste and the bowl is greased or lined with plastic wrap prior to application of the pulp.

The second method, termed 'laminate casting', uses preformed sheets of paper couched directly onto a board. Tear off small pieces of this paper while it is still damp and apply them to the greased bowl, overlapping the torn feathery edges. After two or three layers of these overlapping pieces have been applied, the bowl is left to dry. The bowl is then sprayed with methyl cellulose or painted with a dilute solution of wallpaper paste. Depending on the thickness required, a further two or three layers of overlapping paper strips may be applied. The bowl is dried again and then sealed well with wallpaper paste. Bear

Torn pieces of damp, freshly formed paper, applied to a smooth, greased surface.

A paper bowl made by laminating small pieces of freshly formed paper onto a woven basket.

in mind that if you want to paint the bowl, this must be done before the paste is applied, or the paint will not spread well.

It is possible to apply both of these methods to any curved surface, such as woven baskets, balls, balloons, colanders, casserole dishes or plates. Remember to grease or line the surface that will be covered with the paper and not to remove the paper cast until it is dry. To remove, simply slide a blunt knife between the bowl until the vacuum is broken. Lift the cast off the bowl and paint or seal the inside with wallpaper paste for strength.

Papier-mâché

A book on paper arts and crafts would not be complete without mentioning papier-mâché. The art of making objects from papier-mâché. has existed about as long as paper-making and probably also originated with the Chinese, who used papier-mâché. to create images used in religious festivals. In Europe it gained popularity in the Victorian period, when it was used to make decorative and resilient household articles such as boxes, trays, shelves and furniture. These were finished with several layers of paint and glossy lacquers.

The term paper-mâché originally meant 'made of pulped paper' or literally 'chewed paper', which is now termed mash. Nowadays, it has come to include making paper objects by pasting several layers of torn paper strips onto a mold until the required strength and thickness is achieved.

Today, many articles are still made of papier-mâché: folders, dolls, stage masks and props, and scenery for electric train sets, among others. Artists have re-acquainted themselves with papier-mâché as a sculpting medium, often in combination with painting, acrylics, embroidery and other popular handcrafts.

This section will mainly cover papier-mâché. in its original sense, as 'pulped paper', with a brief outline of the more commonly known method, that of pasting torn strips of paper onto a mold.

Papier-mâché using torn strips

Any kind of paper suitable for making paper pulp will also be suitable for papier-mâché. The paper should be torn and not cut, as torn paper has softer edges, making the overlaps less obvious. Many books on papier-mâché suggest using newspaper, but because of the method of processing the fibers, newspaper is sometimes prone to acid attack and is best avoided for long-lasting articles. The object you use for a mold should be smooth-sided, such as a bowl, plate or ball.

REQUIREMENTS
Torn paper strips
Premixed wallpaper paste
Shallow bowl
Smooth object for a mold
Vaseline

Tear several sheets of paper into small strips and soak these in water. Spread Vaseline over the surface of the mold, or spray it with non-stick baking spray. Build up a layer of paper on the mold, overlapping the strips. The first layer is applied without paste, to prevent the paper from sticking to the mold when dry. When the first layer is complete, paint it with wallpaper paste. Then apply the second layer, painting the inside surface of each strip prior to applying it to the previous layer. You could use different colors for the successive layers, as this makes it easy to see whether the whole area has been covered. Paste three or four layers of paper and then place the object in a warm place to dry.

When dry, paste on another three or four layers, until the desired thickness is reached. Leave to dry in a warm place for a few days. To release your papier-mâché object, slide a blunt knife between the paper and the mold and work it around the edge until it comes free. Don't try to hurry this step or you could tear the papier-mâché. To finish the object, you can give it a fine sandpapering to remove rough edges. Seal the object by painting it with wallpaper paste. An attractive alternative is to give it two coats of paint (artists' gouache, oil paints, or acrylics), followed by a coat of clear matte varnish.

Mash

This method is particularly suited to modelling face masks or pressing into plaster of Paris molds. It has even been used to make furniture. Mash usually needs a basic supporting structure such as modelled clay or carved polystyrene. Supporting molds can also be made from crumpled tinfoil or bent chicken wire. A first layer of torn paper strips laid over the wire or foil acts as a foundation for the mash. Mash can also be applied to a permanent construction, such as the skeleton of a chair, bowl, doll etc., the foundation remaining inside or under the layer of mash.

REQUIREMENTS
One bucket of prepared pulp
Net bag or nylon stocking
Premixed wallpaper paste
Mold
Vaseline

Drain the bucket of pulp through a stocking or net bag, squeezing until it is almost dry. Add one cup of wallpaper paste and boil the pulp and paste until it is tacky and smooth and the water content is reduced. This makes the mash stiffer and easier to model. Grease the surface to be modelled (if you intend to remove it from the cast when the mash is dry) and then spread the mash over it, pressing firmly with your hands. As dried mash tends to have a slightly lumpy appearance, 'buttering' it with a spatula or pressing it with a spoon will result in a smoother surface. However, because of the rough texture of dried mash, you may prefer to create a reverse mold into which to press the mash. A plaster of Paris casting of the object, such as a face mask, works well.

> **Note:** *While papier-mâché resembles the previously outlined techniques such as laminate and paper-casting, there are subtle differences. In the case of papier-mâché the mash is created by boiling up thick pulp with paste until it is stiff and tacky, while the casting techniques described above use pulp that is simply drained. The addition of paste is optional. Laminate casting uses torn strips of freshly formed paper, relying on the bonding properties of the cellulose in the fibers to glue the strips together, while papier-mâché uses dry, ready-made paper strips to which paste is applied.*

Other people's work

An increasing number of artists today are experimenting with paper as an art medium, either on its own or with other media. While several contemporary artists have been exploring the three-dimensional quality of paper in their art, it is beyond the scope of this book to represent them all. However, this section shows a few striking examples of the versatility and flexibility of paper by a few talented artists who specialize in a particular aspect of paper art.

Karlien de Haas (age 6) *The Rainbow* (12½" x 8¾")
Karlien designed this work and chose the colors herself. The idea behind the piece was a landscape which included a rainbow. She began with the rainbow, pouring thin pulp onto an 8½" x 11" mold and the flowers and landscape were added later in thicker pulp. Bright flowers were crayoned in as a finishing touch. As Karlien is left-handed, her signature reads from right to left, rather than the other way around.

Heleen de Haas *Broken diagonal* (25¼" x 19¼")
Heleen works with thick pulp in bright colors, pouring them onto a large silkscreen. She enjoys working with the tactile dimension of the pulp and describes her work as being a combination of painting and sculpture — the pulp can either be fairly fluid and applied like a wash, or used very thick and manipulated like clay. This method is described on page 84.

Heleen de Haas
Heleen's method of working, pouring the pulp directly onto the upper surface of a fine-gauge silkscreen is clearly shown on the right.

Rose Denovan *Bay of tranquility* (22½" x 27¼")
Rose worked with several bowls of colored pulp, built up on a grooved board to make this piece. Once dry, the paper was removed and worked further. The cliffs were drawn with oil crayon while the white waves were painted with gouache.

Rose Denovan *Seen through lace curtains*
The detail above includes both paper-making and embroidery. The paper was poured onto a board and packed with fabric for strength. Once dry the piece was embroidered by hand and machine.

Lin Kerr *How can one buy or sell the air* (20" x 16")
Lin is both a paper-maker and calligrapher and these skills are used to best advantage in this striking piece. She used natural materials such as palm fibers, wool and cotton thread, and gelatine sizing, to create a 'woven carpet' look in earthy colors.

Further reading

Paper-making

Barrett, T. *Japanese Papermaking — Traditions, Tools and Techniques*, Weatherhill, New York and Tokyo, 1983.

Bell, Lilian A. *Plant Fibers for Papermaking*, Liliaceae Press, McMinnville, Oregon, 1988.

Heller, J. *Paper-making*, Watson-Guptill, New York, 1978.

Hughes, S. *Washi, the World of Japanese Paper*, Kodansha International, Tokyo, 1978.

Hunter, D. *Papermaking: The History and Technique of an Ancient Craft*, Dover Publications, New York, 1978.

Richardson, M. *Plant Papers*, Berrington Press, Hereford, 1986.

Stearns, Lynn. *Papermaking for Basketry*, Press de LaPlantz, Inc., Bayside, California, 1988.

Studley, V. *The Art and Craft of Handmade Paper*, Studio Vista, London, 1987.

Toale, Bernard. *The Art of Papermaking*, Davis Publications, Inc., Worcester, Massachusetts, 1983.

Paper and other related crafts

Ashman, J. *Bookbinding, A Beginner's Manual*, A & C Black Ltd., London, 1981.

Banister, M. *Bookbinding as a Handcraft*, Sterling Publishers Inc., New York, 1975.

Bussi, Cathy. *Pressed Flowers, A Creative Guide*, New Holland (Publishers), London, 1988.

Chambers, Anne. *A Practical Guide to Marbling Paper*, Thomas & Hudson, London, 1986.

Green, P. *Introducing Surface Printing*, Batsford Ltd., London, 1967.

Kenny C. and J. *Design in Papier-Mâché*, Pitman & Sons, London, 1973.

Maile, Anne. *Tie-dyed Paper*, Mills & Boon Ltd., London, 1975.

Pretorius, Anika. *Gifts from the Home, A Creative Book of Ideas for Giving*, New Holland (Publishers), London, 1989.

Shannon, Faith. *Paper Pleasures*, Mitchell Beazley, London, 1987.

Strose, S. *Potato Printing*, Sterling, New York, 1968.

Dryad Craft Centre
Hand Paper-making Equipment
178 Kensington High Street
London W8 7RG, England

Falkiner Fine Papers Ltd.
Fine Handmade Papers
76 Southampton Row
London WC1B 4AR, England

Wookey Hole Caves and Papermill
Handmade Papers
New Wells
Somerset, England

Carriage House Paper
Brickbottom
1 Fitchburg Street, #C-207
Somerville, MA 02143

Gold's Artworks Inc.
2100 N. Pine Street
Lumberton, NC 28358

Lee S. McDonald Inc.
Fine Hand Paper-making Equipment
P.O. Box 264
Charlestown, MA 02129

Rugg Road Papers
1 Fitchburg Street
Somerville, MA 02143

Sax Arts and Crafts
P.O. Box 51710
New Berlin, WI 53151

Twinrocker
Handmade Paper and Paper-making Supplies
P.O. Box 413
Brookston, IN 47923

Hand Papermaking (Journal)
P.O. Box 10571
Minneapolis, MN 55458

Index